PSYCHODRAMA
AND
SYSTEMIC THERAPY

Other titles in the

Systemic Thinking and Practice Series

edited by David Campbell & Ros Draper
published and distributed by Karnac Books

Credit Card orders, Tel: 0171-584-3303; Fax: 0171-823-7743

PSYCHODRAMA AND SYSTEMIC THERAPY

Chris Farmer

Foreword by
Zerka T. Moreno

Systemic Thinking and Practice Series

Series Editors
David Campbell & Ros Draper

London
KARNAC BOOKS

First published in 1995 by
H. Karnac (Books) Ltd.
58 Gloucester Road
London SW7 4QY

British Library Cataloguing in Publication Data

A catalogue record for this book is available from the British Library.

ISBN 1 85575 089 9

Printed in Great Britain by BPC Wheatons Ltd, Exeter

ACKNOWLEDGEMENTS

I am grateful to Marcia Karp and Ken Sprague, who introduced me to psychodrama at the Holwell Centre for Psychodrama and Sociodrama, in North Devon, England, where I did most of my training; I also owe much to the work done there with my fellow trainees.

With regard to family and systems therapy in Guernsey, I am particularly indebted to those who have visited the Island to lead workshops. They include John Byng-Hall, Rosalind Draper, and Max Van Trommel. A workshop undertaken in Guernsey by Francis Batten also enhanced the standing of psychodrama in the Island.

The application of systems theory to psychodrama was first presented to me by Anthony Williams at a bicentenary conference in Australia, and its influence has been crucial to my work.

I owe my understanding of Bowen's theory and practice to Marcia Geller at the Carmel Family Therapy Center, New York; with her, I also gained particular experience in working psychodramatically with families.

I thank Olivia Lousada for my interest in the importance of the dynamics involved in the selection of protagonists.

I am very thankful to Lisa King for her secretarial assistance, and to Peter Le Vasseur and Angie Parker for the illustrations.

For the clinical material upon which the book is based, I am greatly indebted to the staff and patients with whom I have worked in Guernsey.

CONTENTS

EDITORS' FOREWORD

W e are very pleased to publish this book, as the way that Dr Farmer looks at the interface of systemic thinking and practice and psychodrama represents, we believe, some original work. It is our hope that both systemic practitioners and drama therapists alike, as well as other mental health professionals, will find the exploration of the relationship between the two perspectives and treatment interventions exciting and stimulating.

The reader will, we hope, appreciate the skills with which Dr Farmer describes his synthesizing of the two approaches and at the same time is able to clarify their distinctiveness.

For many years Dr Farmer has developed the use of a systemic approach to adult mental health problems amongst multidisciplinary staff groups in Guernsey, Channel Islands. During the past few years we have met and worked with Dr Farmer both on the mainland at workshops and conferences that we convened and on Guernsey and Jersey as the interest there in systemic thinking and practice has developed. At the same time, Dr Farmer has gained an international reputation in the field of psychodrama. It is our hope as editors that this book will enthuse practitioners to explore the interface and relationship among a variety of systemic interventions in mental health, thus creating both a rich exchange of ideas and an opportunity for new ideas to emerge.

In the meantime, Dr Farmer's book demonstrates ably through the presentation of well-thought-through ideas and clinical examples what a dedicated clinician can do in the complex environment of psychiatry in adult mental health.

David Campbell
Ros Draper
London
September 1995

FOREWORD

Zerka T. Moreno

Pioneers must be people who rush in where angels fear to tread. So it was with J. L. Moreno when he entered the field of what would later be called "family therapy" and published his first report on his work in *Sociometry, A Journal of Interpersonal Relations*, in 1937. The title of the report was "Inter-personal Therapy and the Psychopathology of Inter-personal Relations". It dealt especially with marital pairs and also with a marital triangle. It was also the first time that the term "auxiliary ego"—the therapist as go-between in the therapeutic process—was used and the functions described. Several segments of psychodramas with the marital partners were included.

It should be remembered that in the 1930s this type of intervention ran counter to all the accepted forms of psychotherapy then being practised, and the amount of resistance to Moreno's ideas was enormous. But one of the earliest persons involved in what became family therapy was Nathan Ackerman. Trained as a psychoanalyst, he met Moreno in the early 1940s and produced his first article in the field of group psychotherapy, for our journal, *Group Psychotherapy*, in 1951. It was called "Psychoanalysis and Group

Psychotherapy". While not yet speaking of family therapy as such, Ackerman wrote:

> The two-person psychoanalytic relationship provides a unique experience in which the earlier patterns of child–parent relations are relived and their destructive elements removed. Group Psychotherapy, involving three or more persons, however, has its dynamic base in the fact that the child's character is influenced, not only by the mother, but all the interacting relationships within the family group, especially the relationship between the parents. These multiple interpersonal patterns, each affecting the other, also contribute to the distortion of personality.

In psychodrama, these interpersonal, interactional patterns are explored in action, not merely analysed, and redirected in action. To indicate how much resistance Ackerman also met when he ventured into the group psychotherapy arena, he wrote in the above-named article:

> At a luncheon meeting of the American Orthopsychiatric Association, at which the plan for the American Group Therapy Association was launched, I timidly suggested that a study of the process of Group Psychotherapy might provide a natural setting for the acquisition of sorely needed knowledge in a new science, social psychopathology. My remark was not then received with favor, but I still cling to that same prejudice. I believe careful study of the process of group psychotherapy may yet give substance to the now-emerging science of social psychopathology.

It is easy to see how Ackerman was drawn to Moreno's ideas and how he began to take steps that culminated, some years later, in the organization of the Ackerman Institute for Family Therapy in New York City.

Since then, group psychotherapy and psychodrama have both become accepted procedures in many areas of interpersonal and inter- and intragroup conflict, with family therapy a firmly established branch. Dr Chris Farmer is here, and in the sequel to this book, presenting a very thorough overview of the many ways he has been able to use psychodrama in a number of settings.

It strikes me that perhaps the term "psychotherapy" itself should be revised. Are we certain that we heal psyches? Moreno was of the opinion that psyches are particularly difficult to influence. He felt that it was relationships that do the influencing, and it was through relationships that healing might take place. Should we start calling ourselves "relationship therapists"? It was especially with the sociometric system that Moreno was concerned as the basis for charting, diagnosing, and changing interpersonal relations. Sociometry has been difficult for psychiatrists to grasp, coming, as they do, from medical training and the concern for one particular individual at a time. It took a long time for the idea to penetrate that all human relations are involved in psychotherapy. Moreno placed sociometry as the umbrella under which group psychotherapy and psychodrama fell. He thought that it was basic to group psychotherapy and psychodrama to understand the underlying human relations, which sociometry—the measurement of human relations—could best reveal, like a microscope on the group, whereas psychodrama was the microscope of the psyche with its interrelations. Most psychotherapists who use group psychotherapy and psychodrama have lifted these approaches from under the umbrella. Dr Chris Farmer has made splendid use of sociometry as well as role theory and presents the kind of systems thinking and operations that form the ground of his own work. Although literature on psychodrama is proliferating in many languages, this use of social systems is still fairly rare, and therefore this book is a contribution to what is still, in many ways, a pioneering effort.

Beacon, New York

PREFACE

C omplex social interaction within a small and clearly defined geographical area provides fertile ground for a systems therapist and for a psychodrama practitioner who works with families.

In a small community, to be close to the action is to be provided with a multiplicity of perspectives from which to view the evolution of family systems. Guernsey, having a relatively dense population within a well-defined physical boundary, contains a high degree of complexity with regard to the interrelationships of its residents. Family stories extend over long periods of time and in one place, enabling clinical material to be put into context, both historically and contemporaneously. The closer an observer is to the action, the more specific the information that is received; it is what is particular that is of importance when it comes to defining differences—a task necessary for learning about complex interaction. What is specific, however, is defined in relation to what is general, and what is general is, in turn, an abstraction from similarities. Psychodrama explicitly addresses the specific: "Who?", "What?", "Where?", or "When?"—these are the questions that enable the stage to be set.

The scene, however, is also a group-therapy room, and the cast are group members, or perhaps are symbolized by chairs; their meaning is determined by what or whom they refer to, specifically, in the minds of those present. Specificity, however, does not require a faithful transcription of all phenomena so much as a portrayal of the relationships among them. The most specific of all personal information—the names of people and places—have been changed throughout this book to preserve confidentiality, and the stories have been fictionalized sufficiently to render their subjects unidentifiable.

This book is about linking systemic thought with action in psychiatry. It consists of descriptions in the form of narratives—my own accounts of other people's stories. Similarly, as observers, systems therapists and psychodrama practitioners also address the observations of other observers. Different clinicians could have told different stories concerning the same case material reported in this book. The patients and relatives, yet again, might have covered the same ground with different narratives of their own. There is, however, an important distinction between narratives that are deliberately invented to illustrate an idea—regarded as "true" only in a mythical sense—and those that are written as an historical document. Even so, history can be regarded as a record of selected observations.

If, in systems terms, what is more complex can help to explain what is simpler, it is essential to decide what to include and what to leave out to prevent the description itself from becoming too intricate to be comprehensible. The selection is personal and subjective; in keeping with a social constructionist view of "reality", the material can be regarded as a map (my own version) of other maps. Also, all narratives require selectivity with regard to what is left out. If everything that happened were reported, there would not be "history"; there would be but a record without meaning or interpretation. The historian, like the family therapist, must punctuate data to provide useful information. In real life, events in themselves do not have beginnings or ends. These are marked according to where people choose to define them. While aiming to preserve the authenticity of the material by referring to sequences of events and to patterns of clinical and family interaction, this selective process also serves to safeguard the confidentiality of the people who were involved by making them unrecognizable.

* * *

In a sequel to this book, the themes are elaborated in more complicated stories that include work carried out with different generations of families over extended periods of time, yet within the context of the same public health service. Case histories may refer as far back in time as one is able to record; it might be thought that the Second World War would have acted as a suitable historical limit in time to the events covered, yet the very features of the Occupation and the Evacuation figure significantly in the case material, and the stories continue after the writing of this book.

PSYCHODRAMA
AND
SYSTEMIC THERAPY

Introduction

oreno, the pioneer of interpersonal relations in the fields of sociometry, group therapy, psychodrama, and sociodrama, entered the domain of family therapy when he published "Inter-personal Therapy and the Psychopathology of Inter-personal Relations" (Moreno, 1937a). As Compernolle (1981) points out, Moreno had in 1973 presented formulations of a true systems orientation, but he is not widely mentioned in the literature of systemic therapy. I believe this to be in part because he had developed his own language of interpersonal relations and therapeutic techniques, to cover wider areas than family therapy, before the advent of General Systems Theory and its influence upon the thinking of later family and systems therapists. He has been most widely known as the originator of psychodrama, which until recent years was not appreciated in terms of systems theory.

A full and definitive exposition of psychodrama as a systemic therapy was undertaken by Williams (1989) when he defined its techniques and its rationale in the language of systems and cybernetics. It was also pointed out by Chasin, Roth, and Bograd (1989), who described a means to employ action techniques in post-Milan

1

systemic interviewing, that action methods of various kinds have had a rich tradition in family therapy. Tomm (1991) has developed the technique of encouraging patients to speak from the "inner voice" of family members by asking "internalized other questions". It resembles a psychodramatic technique, such as role-reversal, except that there is no physical interaction.

One overall view of therapy as change concerns the association between belief, perception, and behaviour; what we believe is affected by what we see, which, in turn, depends upon what behaviour is taking place. Likewise, our beliefs affect the way we see the world—how we draw distinctions by creating meaningful differences between the phenomena that we perceive (Bateson, 1979). Our interpretation of events, in turn, affects our behaviour (Campbell, Draper, & Huffington, 1989).

In this way, our beliefs, and thus our behaviour, can be viewed as arising from the way we see the world and by the meaning that we attach to phenomena. Such a recursive pattern implies that our beliefs are socially created, or—in the language of social psychology—"constructed" (Kelly, 1955).

Psychodrama can be regarded as a medium for proliferating perspectives and making available multiple ways of defining phenomena. It is co-constructed (Anderson, Goolishian, & Windermand, 1987) by the protagonist, the director, and the group, and it allows for a multitude of possible scenarios to be explored. It is grounded in action, and it allows behaviour to be experienced at different levels and viewed from many angles by both the observers and the subjects of the action. As experience and perception affect belief, which, in turn, influences behaviour, psychodrama, by incorporating the ideas, perceptions, and behaviour of many people besides those of the protagonist, provides recursive loops that reflexly influence the relationships between belief, perceptions, and behaviour.

Psychodrama exploits the abundance of possible ideas, feelings, and actions to create opportunities to determine the manner by which these can be interrelated. Instead of separating phenomena or beliefs into dualities or pluralities, systemic thinking involves seeking the connection between apparently independent phenomena or ideas and subsuming them into an overall pattern that includes dichotomies and distinctions at a higher level of organization or from a wider viewpoint (Fruggeri & Matteini, 1991).

In this way, the events and experiences in a psychodrama are set into a context from which they can more readily be defined and understood. Psychodrama is par excellence a "marker of contexts" (Boscolo, Cecchin, Campbell, & Draper, 1985) insofar as the stage is precisely the place to create and shift contexts. Furthermore, as a co-creative endeavour, it allows for socially assembled meanings to emerge from the interaction of belief, perception, and behaviour.

My ideas about psychiatry and therapy were influenced by the position that I adopted as a practising medical clinician. This, in turn, affected the appointments I took and the way that I worked. This book is an account of the application of systemic thinking to the understanding of psychodrama and of how I apply each of these approaches to general psychiatric practice.

The ideas developed as my work as a psychiatrist began to cover a variety of treatment modalities from a traditional medical approach, through various individual and group psychotherapy models, to a way of conceptualizing mental health care that incorporates different theoretical perspectives and styles of working.

This development of thought and methods of working went hand in hand as theory and practice co-evolved through their mutual interaction, and it led me to reflect upon the relationship of one to the other.

I see psychiatric work as involving both an individual doctor–patient dialogue and various models of multiple interaction that include, for example, a team of staff colleagues, families, groups of patients (in a therapeutic milieu), and various agencies. To avoid splitting and pluralism, there has to be an approach to conceptualizing these different methods in such a way that they are connected through one unified presentation that encompasses them all. This must apply both to the psychiatric service and to the individual people (staff, family members, and patients), so that each of the ways of working has a relationship to the others. For a number of years I have carried two titles: "Consultant Psychiatrist" and "Consultant Psychotherapist"; one applies to my status and the tasks I am expected to perform, and the other refers to particular ways in which I work. I have been happy to retain both titles in that I would not wish to have only one of them without the other.

Systemic thinking began to be helpful to me when I worked with families. Later, it also enabled me to link together other ways of working with patients, staff, families, and referring agencies. After reading a paper by Fruggeri and Matteini (1991), "therapy" in a state-run system of mental health care began for me to have a distinctive meaning according to the context of the service in which the "therapy" was carried out: the mental health service could operate "therapeutically" if the way the methods of mental health care were thought about had an effect upon how the service functioned and vice versa. Psychodrama is regarded as a method of treating an individual and a group concurrently. It is, therefore, a paradigm for the task of keeping in mind simultaneously both what is specific to individual people and what is in common with others, be it a particular diagnostic category, an inevitable life problem (such as grief), or the experience of being a member of a family, a patient in an acute ward or day unit, a staff member of a particular discipline, or a participant in group therapy.

Psychodrama, more than any other medium that I employ, addresses the need to conceptualize individuality and generality at the same time. It illustrates ways of thinking systemically, and it can, in itself and in its own right, be regarded as a form of systemic therapy that eminently allows for dove-tailing with other therapeutic media.

In writing about psychodrama as a systemic therapy, therefore, I shall also be referring to ways of using systemic thinking in the general management of patients in a state-run mental health service.

This is not a book about psychiatry as such, nor is it a treatise on systemic thinking as applied to family therapy or consultation (for which see Campbell et al., 1989, and Jones, 1993). Neither is it a manual or treatise on psychodrama, for which I suggest Blatner and Blatner (1988), Goldman and Morrison (1984), Kipper (1986), and Kellermann (1992). For the distillation of the writings of the founder of psychodrama, J. L. Moreno, I refer to *The Essential Moreno* (Fox, 1987) and for a recently published account of the use of psychodrama in the treatment of a family, undertaken by J. L. Moreno and Zerka T. Moreno, I recommend the chapter "Time, Space, Reality, and the Family", written by Zerka Moreno, the greatest living exponent of J. L. Moreno's work, in Holmes and Karp (1991).

The definitive exposition of the most modern practice of psycho-drama is to be found in *Psychodrama Since Moreno* (Holmes, Karp, & Watson, 1994).

It is assumed that the reader is already acquainted with systems theory, though this does not presuppose any prior knowledge of psychodrama.

The psychodrama sessions described in this book involved groups of between twelve and twenty-two participants, including two nursing staff, plus the director; 20% of patients were from the ward, and the remainder were day patients. In most sessions, approximately 60% of patients were female. Ages varied from 16 to 65.

I begin with a history of my experience in psychiatry and in working with different ideas about therapy. I then focus upon a description of psychodrama in systemic language. Later I provide illustrations with narratives using psychodramatic material. Finally, in discussing how psychodrama relates to other aspects of patient care I examine ways of thinking systemically about psychiatric care in general.

CHAPTER ONE

Psychiatry systems and drama

SYSTEMIC FAMILY THERAPY

Family therapy looks at the system as it appears to the therapist and to the family members as they interact in a session. I say "it appears" because "it" does not exist, except in the minds of the individual members. Each member and therapist would regard the system from a different viewpoint; if it were a psychodrama and not a family therapy session, each would present his own distinct individual representation of the family. There is no "correct" portrayal. The "family system" is an abstraction that is derived from each individual's perceptions and formulations as these evolve together in the minds of the family members and the therapists while they participate together in dialogue (Anderson et al., 1987).

Systemic family therapy seeks to enable the family to define itself in such a way as is congruent for the individual members. The feedback gained from such techniques as circular and reflexive questioning helps each person to see himself more clearly in relation to other family members. Together they utilize the knowledge of differences that feedback provides to construct a redefinition of the family system that encompasses the descriptions of each individual member. Thus, at the end of a period of systemic family therapy, one would in theory expect that if each individual member were to enact a psychodrama, it would portray a family picture that is more akin to that of other family members than it would have been before family therapy began.

This, of course, is the ideal—that family members would have recognized shared meanings about how their family should operate and would then have interpreted the attitudes and behaviour of each other in accordance with their beliefs. Such belief systems, however, are not static; when recognized and expressed in dialogue, the shared configurations of belief evolve as the family members seek to incorporate their different ideas into a more all-embracing pattern of meaning. Like a "figure" in gestalt psychology, beliefs never stay the same; as they are apprehended, they merge into the "ground" from which they had arisen and are replaced in the perception of the subject by different images.

For a family system to survive and develop, it needs to have access to, and to utilize information from, the wider social system of which it is a part and which itself is subject to flux.

The family boundary is permeable to a varying degree, but entry, growth, and separation or death is inevitable. As a family evolves through time, beliefs change to accommodate to transitions in its life cycle and to the vicissitudes of society outside the family. Furthermore, individual members become more differentiated from their original family beliefs as they adapt themselves to life outside. Were people to view themselves the same way in their relationships outside the family as they do inside, it is likely that neither they nor their family could develop appropriately. If family members share and accept each other's individual development, they can evolve together with relatively congruent ideas; if they can accept differences and yet stay connected, they do not have to split off their individuality from their family life, and the other family members also can develop their own autonomy.

What is important is a unity (but not a uniformity) that allows for differences. The ideal family model for systemic therapists includes a shared belief about allowing for or encouraging individuality within a framework of members belonging together but respecting differences. This I will term a meta-belief of systemic therapists: the notion that family members can be different and have different beliefs but still be connected, be attached, or "belong" to one another in some way.

If systemic family therapy seeks to avoid the limitations of treating one member rather than the family as a whole, then it might appear that psychodramas by individuals about family problems would be a contradiction to family therapy. Both media, however, promote differentiation of self. Thus, while psychodrama has everything to do with individuality, it is also a group activity and is grounded in communality. In fact, it is the very structure and rules of a psychodrama group that enable a person to find his individuality.* Whether we are in family groups or in stranger groups, our selves evolve in relationship; it is through the process of interacting that we develop and become aware of ourselves as individuals. Moreover, we can only comprehend differences if there are also similarities from which the differences can be distinguished (Agazarian, 1993). We grow as families and as individuals through both identification and differentiation.

PSYCHODRAMA

In addition to presenting dramatic action on the stage, psychodrama exemplifies the dramatic quality of human interaction in general in the way that people relate to one another and then reflect upon their exchanges. [Throughout the book, I refer to psychodrama in a clinical context and in relation to its direct use in elucidating and resolving problems that relate to present or past family situations.] In life we are constantly engaging dramatically with one another when we encounter each other in defined situations. Our personal narratives are of news and not of routines. Stories require the interruption of routines (Johnstone, 1979). What becomes meaningful and interesting is the way connections are made between otherwise commonplace or predictable events. Our life stories are about the interaction of the expected with the unexpected—the stuff of comedy and tragedy. Hopes become dashed, or

---

*Throughout, in general situations "he" is used for both masculine and feminine pronouns to keep the text as clear and as uncluttered as possible.

they are fulfilled despite obstacles. We are all dramatic insofar as we think of ourselves in dramatic terms; we are aware of being observed or experienced by those with whom we interact (Brittan, 1973). Together we each conspire to create in life our own roles of victim and tyrant, loser and winner, and so on. This is also the language of staged drama.

Analytic psychotherapy is a dialogue. For some people, it is sufficient in itself to gain access to feelings and to link them with thoughts to find meaning. Others also require action; they express themselves non-verbally to "show" as well as to "tell". Everyday gestures indicate how we express ourselves in movement—in space as well as in time. As an amateur pianist, I am very much aware that music I "remember" is not "in my head" in a form in which it can be written on manuscript paper; it is recalled as I use my hands. Without the movement of my hands on the keyboard, I would not even "know" that I remembered the details of the music. Thus from action I learn from myself as well as about myself.

Moreover, with action I can put a narrative into a frame of reference without having to contextualize my conversation with additional language. Action can put words into a framework without the use of yet more words as meta-dialogue. Conversely, words can be the index of action: if the content of a communication is words, then action is the process, and vice versa. In drama, the index of context and the context itself occur simultaneously with an immediacy that establishes an impact upon both actors and observers.

Movement also changes the circumstances of the actor as observer of himself. As a pianist hears his music while his fingers are operating, so the self-reflective actor experiences himself roused as he acts. Insofar as he sees the same scene differently as he changes position, he experiences the others on the stage in a novel aspect.

There are important differences between the contexts of psychodrama and family therapy. Psychodrama is usually a stranger-group activity, even though it is very often about families, whereas family therapy involves people who already belong to a well-organized and long-established human group. The implications of this distinction are considerable. A protagonist would never express himself in a family group in the way he does on the psychodrama stage, where he has the freedom to present himself without the external constraints of the other family members; he does not have to consider their feelings or to be accountable to them afterwards—he can return to his family without them knowing what took place.

However, even without family members being present, he is still subject to substantial constraints pertaining to the influence of his family; they appear to be experienced largely as coming from within himself if, indeed, he is even aware of them. Psychodrama can help him look at the limitations he imposes upon himself. It explores the family system that he has internalized (Holmes, 1992; Laing, 1967).

Psychodrama is a medium par excellence for both identification and for differentiation. The first phase is termed the "warm-up" and consists of simple group procedures that enable the members to make contact with one another. They share their sense of being together as they become aware of their similarities and differences. Sub-grouping may be encouraged to highlight areas of similarities of interest, energy, or feeling (Fig. 1.1). Differences between sub-groups may then be compared with differences within sub-groups (Agazarian, 1993). Eventually there emerges a group concern that becomes centred upon the topic of the psychodrama and the selection of the protagonist for the action phase.

Drama elicits identification, whether it is in "life" or upon the stage. The actor needs to recognize his rapport with the audience, and the members of the audience in turn put themselves in the shoes of the actor. Staged drama allows for maximum identification between actors and audience in both directions. The spectators sympathize with the victim, hate the persecutor, and become excited as combatants fight. The actors, in turn, are aware of the spectators' emotional involvement with them. The "stage" need not be in the theatre—it can be a sporting event, a chess contest, or even a scenario in front of a real kitchen sink. Wherever the actual drama takes place, however, the process follows certain universal patterns, such as, for example, contests in which there are winners and losers. The distinctive difference with the theatre is that the outcome has been arranged in advance of the action.

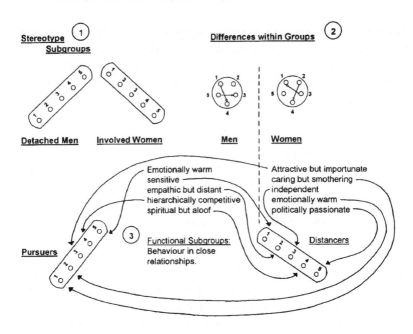

FIGURE 1.1

A psychodrama is usually a story, and so it has a beginning, a middle, and an end. It is not a routine, and, unlike a play in the theatre, the end is not known to anyone until it has been reached. The middle is the breaking-up of set patterns. The story is that of the protagonist. It evolves as it happens on the stage. Nothing is pre-ordained. It is not planned in advance. The protagonist usually has a general idea of what he wants to do, but neither the protagonist nor anyone else will know how scenes will be experienced and how people will respond until the actual episodes come to pass.

This is not to say that there is no structure. There is a psychodramatic process, which the director follows to enable the protagonist to find his way to tell his story. The director has rules and techniques to allow the protagonist to attain the required roles and then, in portraying them, to feel, to act, and to think. Insight and understanding come through integration of experience shared with other group members.

PSYCHODRAMA AS A SYSTEMS THERAPY

The first function of the director is to set boundaries in space and in time (Fig. 1.2). There is a stage, a place for the action. There is a group. There is an overall context—an expectation of dramatic action in the group. There is a time sequence: the warm-up, the action, and the closure with sharing.

With regard to the overall spatial structure, the director attends to a permeable boundary between those on the stage and the other members of the group. He draws upon the members for participation in the scenes, and he scans the group for its response during the action; the audience is an essential participant whose contributions the director taps. Without an audience—either real or implied—as witness to the action, there is no drama.

During the action, the director helps the protagonist to manipulate time and space in the choice of settings and in the starting and finishing of individual scenes. He organizes scenes to take place in the present, even though they may represent the past, a hypothetical future, a "pretend" situation, or an impossible scene (termed "surplus reality"). Scenes initially may portray what "really" hap-

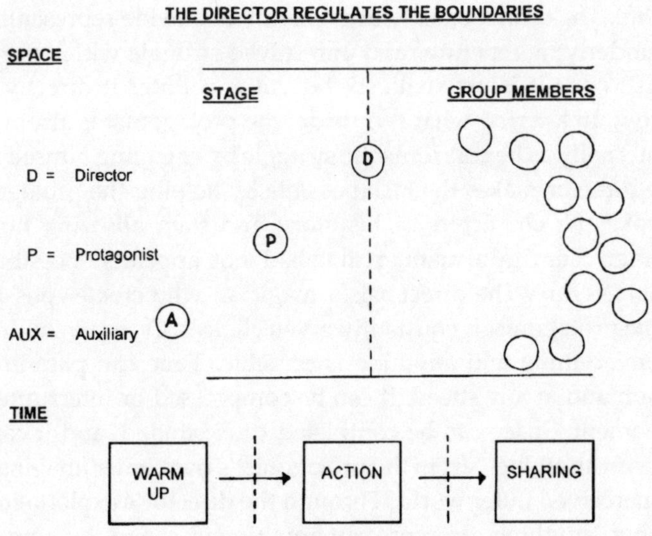

THE DIRECTOR REGULATES THE BOUNDARIES

FIGURE 1.2

pened; later, however, the director is more interested in what did not happen but might or should have taken place.

The director has people from the group act as the "auxiliaries" and take on the roles that represent aspects of the protagonist's life—inside or outside of the boundary of his individual self. Although mainly chosen by the protagonist, they are regarded as tools of the director to help the protagonist to demonstrate himself in his life situation. These auxiliaries typically represent the significant other people in the protagonist's life with whom he enacts his drama. As an example, the action may start in the present day with people at work and then be followed by a family scene in which there is found to be a fundamental and unresolvable conflict of the same pattern. The similarities are explained, and the protagonist has the opportunity to work through the original drama to a more satisfying conclusion. From the experience of achieving this and the process of struggling with the forces within himself that have hitherto been out of contact or awareness, he gains insight and a sense of power. He is able to accomplish this by externalizing what is inside and thus "seeing" and therefore confronting what he has been trying unsuccessfully to grapple with internally. Typically, these patterns of conflict have been internalized during early family life.

The auxiliaries are thus also manifestations of the protagonist's inner life. The drama usually begins with an outside representation of an underlying repetitive and unresolved struggle within the protagonist; once it is externalized, he can encounter it directly and change it. In altering what is outside, the protagonist is also modified internally as he confronts the struggle by engaging himself in it.

The director makes the task possible by helping the protagonist to invoke the characters of his story and then allowing him to encounter them in a manner that had not appeared possible or desirable before. The director is a magician who creates possibilities. The protagonist is constantly given choices. On a psychodrama stage, everything and anything is possible. Time can pass in any direction and at any speed. It can be compressed or interrupted at any moment. Space can be contracted or expanded, and it can be filled with anything—from the protagonist's own inner imagination to his perceived outer world. Through the director's exploitation of metaphor, anything can represent anything else, and, by a process termed "concretization", ideas or images may be put into spatial dimensions in the form of objects or of people on the stage.

The protagonist must apprehend and acknowledge new possibilities, and he must also learn to accept the impossibilities. He must make the choices. The director shows what is conceivable. The protagonist must explore and understand before he can choose, and then he has to choose for himself. To accomplish something hitherto regarded as impossible or undesirable, he must see things in a new way. This is accomplished through action. Instead of passively accepting what is presented to him, he acts, and he invents as he actively creates his own drama. With spontaneity, he wills as he moves, and he discovers as he explores. Finally, in dramatic action, as he experiences, so he becomes. Mental and bodily action become one.

For the protagonist to see new possibilities, the director employs (apart from a multitude of secondary procedures) certain basic techniques that involve the use of other group members in the roles of "auxiliary egos"—tools of the director, used to represent other people in the drama or parts of the patient's self (real or invented). The protagonist, in addition to presenting himself (as he is, was, should have been, wishes to be, etc.) (Fig. 1.3), also steps into the role of the other personalities in the drama as he introduces them to the group. Group members, chosen by the protagonist, then becomes the auxiliaries, taking the roles of the persons portrayed (Fig. 1.4). In these roles, each auxiliary will behave as seems natural to himself as a group member; the protagonist or director can correct an auxiliary if the role is not sufficiently authentic.

As well as the other people in a scene, the director may suggest that the protagonist should have a "double" who stands just beside and behind the protagonist to empathize and to put into words what the protagonist may be feeling but for which he has not yet found a verbal expression (Fig. 1.5). The protagonist has the opportunity to modify or negate what the double has said, but the double has introduced more possibilities. The double, who is experienced as a supportive part of the protagonist, can distance himself just a little from the action and reflect aloud at the same time as the protagonist is acting or speaking; these roles can alternate, so that the double can act or speak while the protagonist reflects.

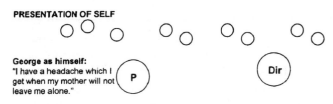

FIGURE 1.3

In another technique, the protagonist steps outside the scene to view it from a distance, while an auxiliary—referred to as a "mirror"—represents the protagonist (Fig. 1.6). The protagonist is thus able to perceive himself and to reflect about, comment upon, or address the mirror. The difference in perspective allows the protagonist to discern more possibilities or options for proceeding with the action. This interaction with the mirror epitomizes the reflexivity (Holland, 1977) of drama. The actor on the stage, typifying the dramatic aspect of the human condition, keeps the audience (real or imagined) in consideration as he performs; with the "mirror", the subject literally steps outside himself, as though into the audience, to visualize his own situation.

The most powerful of all the techniques available to the director is that of role reversal. The protagonist and an auxiliary change places (Fig. 1.7). In the role of the auxiliary, the protagonist interacts with the auxiliary portraying the protagonist. The protagonist, therefore, sees himself through the eyes of the auxiliary and at the

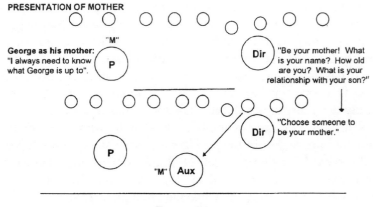

FIGURE 1.4

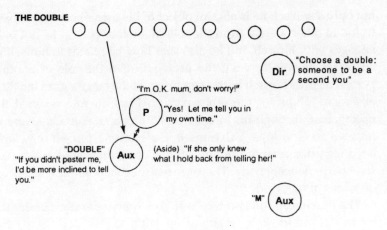

FIGURE 1.5

same time puts himself into the shoes of the auxiliary. Typically, this role reversal is repeated a number of times. Among its many functions—the movement itself intensifies the interaction—it evokes the hitherto unacknowledged and perhaps unfulfilled relationship between the protagonist as subject and the other also as a subject. In other words, it puts into bodily form the protagonist's perception of the other person as a subjective being. In the language of Buber (Inger, 1993), the "I–Thou" relationship, which has been internalized by the protagonist, is given tangible expression as it is depicted on the stage.

Role reversal also addresses the relationship between the protagonist's own subjective and objective selves. The protagonist is

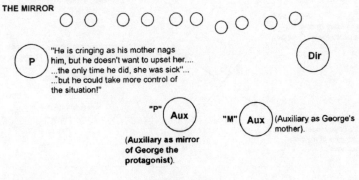

FIGURE 1.6

not only a subject; he is also an object of his own observing subjectivity. In other words, from the role of another person he not only engages with himself, but he also sees how he relates to himself as an object. In role reversal the protagonist in the role of another person regards himself both as an object of the other's gaze (an "It") and as a "Thou" of the other person. Thus, in role reversal the protagonist, through his interaction with others, is made aware of his own relationships with himself. For example, his self may have been regarded as split into an actively observing mind and a passively experiencing body. There are many other possible conceptual divisions of this kind.

The misconception that the "self" is a unity operating under the control of, or in direct relationship with, the "I" (or "ego") has recently been reviewed by Symington (1993), who describes how some of the "inner personalities" or parts of the self can be relatively independent sources of action. The body itself, however, is often conceived of as a "thing" or an "it" (Laing, 1959).

It is an interesting feature of role reversal that a chair or an auxiliary can be brought in to represent the body, a part of the body

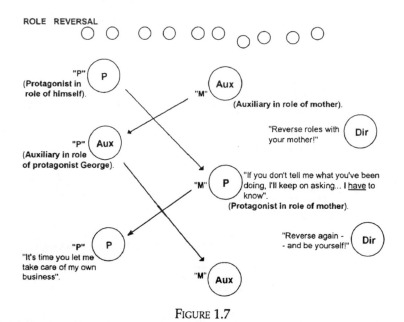

FIGURE 1.7

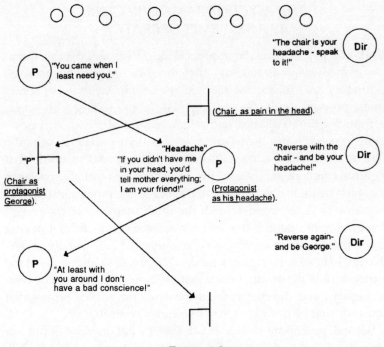

FIGURE 1.8

or an inner self or personality; if the protagonist role-reverses with his "body" (represented by a chair or by an auxiliary), he finds that, as his "body", he can speak to "himself". In other words, he becomes identified with the people and the parts of himself that he invokes, and when externalized on the stage, these parts can engage in dialogue (Fig. 1.8).

To take "mind and body" as an example, these are sometimes regarded as a duality, but in reverse-role they operate as a recursive complementarity (Keeney, 1983). Indeed, the person of the protagonist is more than the sum of mind and body: role reversal can be viewed as a second-order cybernetics. It is no accident that role reversal is regarded as the "engine", powerhouse, or motive force of psychodrama. The interaction becomes more concentrated and dynamic as the role reversal proceeds. The dialogue becomes sharper and the content more specific.

THE PSYCHODRAMA DIRECTOR
AS A SYSTEMIC OPERATOR

While the psychodramatic approach in itself is an effective therapeutic medium, it is the way that the director actually uses the
techniques that makes the method powerful. A scene can sometimes proceed with the protagonist alone setting the stage,
introducing the auxiliaries, and role-reversing with each as the dialogue proceeds; the protagonist, on his own initiative, uses the
medium to explore what he needs to discover and to fulfil what
requires completion. Usually the protagonist eventually becomes
lost. First he finds it very difficult both to be the protagonist and, at
the same time, to negotiate with the other members of the group.
The essence of drama is that one can act and speak without having
to comment upon or qualify what is being said; it is usually preferable not to have to engage in a meta-dialogue. Also, the status of the
protagonist in the group is such that he should not have to be both
protagonist and director at the same time; the role of protagonist
demands that he must be free to relinquish control.

Second, psychodrama is as much about what does not or did not
happen as about what actually happens or happened in life. The
protagonist needs another pair of eyes that sees what is missing
from his own vision.

The director, therefore, punctuates the action. He interrupts. He
extends. He connects what appears separate. Furthermore, as a true
systemic operator, he finds similarities in the apparently different
and differences in the supposedly similar—whether this pertains to
specific samples of the action, such as a symmetrical escalation of
dialogue, or to the overall shape of the drama, where, for example,
he may observe an isomorphic pattern between a present-day office
scene and a childhood family incident.

By stopping the action, by questioning the protagonist, the auxiliaries, or the group, the director clearly is regarded as controlling
the proceedings. It might be thought that the protagonist can hardly
find his individuality under such circumstances. It is, however, the
director's control that allows the protagonist to be aware of what
otherwise are the hidden restraints—to seeing, choosing, acting—
that are within himself or bear upon himself. The meaning of the
word "control" is itself a social construction.

In systemic thought, the notion of physical control of one living thing by another is not considered helpful when it refers to one "making" the other do, think, or feel something. The way an organism responds to stimuli is determined by its own structure (Maturana & Varela, 1980). A protagonist may respond to information if it is presented in a way that is meaningful to him, but whether he responds and how he does so is a matter that depends upon the protagonist himself. The director, in fact, only "controls" what he himself does or says. His "power" comes from the status given to him by the group, one role of which includes an observing stance (Maturana & Varela, 1980). He is the only one who is empowered to walk about the stage independently of the action of the auxiliaries. The group have invested him with the role of a moving observer. The director can choose where to observe from. Furthermore, he can elicit other observations from anyone else in the group or on the stage.

If observations are made by detecting differences, then the director is also searching for new viewpoints from which to discover such differences. In other words, he is also a "meta-observer" of differences. He creates conditions for feedback. As the protagonist and the group, together, acquire new information from fresh sources of feedback, they evolve into a more self-correcting system. It is, then, the protagonist under the conditions of this group system who makes his own connections and who finds his own meaning. The director helps him to find the clues.

The director also helps to make this whole process possible. He, with the permission and cooperation of the group, creates the conditions for psychodrama. He also "marks the context" (Boscolo et al., 1985) as he punctuates the action. He decides when to present more choices to the protagonist or when to help the protagonist to notice when he is avoiding a choice or a commitment to a choice.

Whenever the director interrupts the action, he is making an intervention. He talks to the protagonist, an auxiliary, or perhaps to the group, asking for comments from part of the observing system. A piece of action can be repeated, perhaps in a different way (it can be argued that in a repetition there will not be an exact replication; there will be some difference, which may be used as a resource). The protagonist can be asked what he is experiencing—what he wants from the scene and what is missing. The protagonist also can stop at any time to comment or to talk, as can the auxiliaries. Soliloquy as a theatrical device is also very powerful. It not only conveys "private" thoughts to the group; it also provides time and space for the protagonist to reflect during the middle of a scene or conversation.

It is in the use of metaphor that the director is most imaginative. As previously stated, on the stage anything can represent something else. Where possible, use is made of the protagonist's own symbols, and often these point to the essence of the psychodrama. For example, a protagonist may feel "boxed in" at work. Later another "box" may be found in family life or in childhood experience. The box is created with chairs or with people. This is an instance of the director's use of concretization to make the abstract tangible. The protagonist can converse with the box, reverse-role with it, and physically grapple with it. If the box represents particular people, then auxiliaries can represent them as the protagonist wrestles, using his bodily power, to become in touch with feelings thus far locked inside him and perhaps hitherto unrecognized.

There is another fundamental property of psychodrama that goes to the roots of the relationship between families, religion, and the State. When I began slowly to become involved in psychodrama, its particular attraction for me was its apparent universality, its appeal to what deeply mattered to people, and its power through its vitality and intensity to hold their imagination at a deep level. Like the preaching of John Wesley or the rhetoric of St Paul or of Martin Luther King, it had the influence to touch the hearts and move the spirits of men and women. The clue was the significance of drama and its beginnings in ancient Greece.

Plato was not enthusiastic about drama because of the unbecoming emotions it gave to players of ignoble roles and the base passions it gave to the spectators. Drama was criticized for not being true to life. Others, however, saw that it was precisely the ambiguity between the "as if" and the "real" (the playing with differences!) that drew people to drama. Greek drama is said to have started with the first citizens' jury, who tried Orestes for killing Clytemnestra, his mother (a "courtroom drama" was perhaps the archetypal play!). Instead of having Orestes punished by the avenging Furies, the State took over the responsibility for dealing with the punishment of homicide. Individual and family retribution was given over to the social management of equity. The first plays were adversarial battles over rights and wrongs, responsibilities, and injustices.

It is interesting to remember this historical background in a "courtroom sentencing scene" (a device of modern psychodrama), when a protagonist is given the power to avenge his adversary. Very often this happens when the protagonist is an adult victim of child abuse and is expressing outrage at the perpetrator. Revenge and retribution are no longer the prerogative of family members in the civilized Western world, where such passions are denied expression and justice is at the disposal of the courts.

Nowadays it is not so much the murder of parents by children for which justice is assigned to the institutionalized mediation of the courts; it is decidedly more often the abuse of children by their parents that is supposed to be dealt with by socially established methods of jurisdiction. It is not murdered parents who are unavenged, but injured children who have to assign retribution over to society and who, deprived of an outlet for their rightful anger, are also thereby denied the working-through of their individual grief.

THE CONTEXT FOR CLINICAL PSYCHODRAMA

Despite the universality of dramatic engagement, psychodrama is not itself the epitome of therapy for everyone. Family therapy has addressed the problem of treating in isolation an "identified patient" who is the scapegoat or symptom-bearer for the rest of the family. Psychodrama might often clarify the position if given sufficient information from the protagonist, but it has to contend with the power of a family—particularly one with which a patient is in constant contact—to overcome any efforts of even an insightful and motivated individual to differentiate himself. Furthermore, the reciprocity between the protagonist and the other family members could well entail the latter requiring help in adjusting to the changing pattern of relationships. With a need to modify the universality of psychodrama with the systemic framework of family therapy, breadth as well as depth is required.

In Guernsey, where I work, I have the autonomy to operate in an unconventional way for a consultant psychiatrist in a general adult psychiatric practice. The island also has a very circumscribed population, thus making it possible to make contact with different family members or to follow them up over long periods of time. Another effect of working in a small and well-defined environment is that there are likely to be fewer levels of hierarchy in a therapeutic system. This makes it possible for me to work in and from different positions: in the home of a family, in one-to-one work with an individual, with a multidisciplinary team at ward level, in group therapy and psychodrama, with the courts and care agencies, liaising with the physicians in the hospital, working with the family doctors, the charities, and occasionally at the political level. The significance of exercising choice in terms of the observational field in the area of mental health is pointed out by Telfner (1991).

Working in these various areas, I noticed that different time-spans were appropriate to the various levels in the hierarchical system from which I was operating. If the situation needed immediate attention, it was probably in the family home, where, for example, the children's officer, a family doctor, or the police had been called in, in response to a crisis. The interaction of the two systems—family and agency—required a quick decision, as there was little time for all to be together in the home.

On the ward also, however, the need for a prompt decision might have arisen such as when the nursing staff were required to decide how to manage a patient who had suddenly changed his mind about being a patient. Could such a person be restrained? Was it legal? Was it dangerous? Would the patient come to harm if he left the hospital? These were major decisions, and there was little time to reflect or to engage in dialogue about them.

Unfortunately, such moments often encapsulate in a very short period of time the essence of the problem requiring the patient to be in the ward; the patient might have been attempting to determine the point in time and the length of time over which a decision was to be made. The staff were feeling responsible, but the patient was setting the agenda and demanding action—in other words, a decision. (For a systemic exposition of this dilemma at the ward level, see Mason, 1989.)

This incongruous hierarchy could have resulted from an earlier failure to negotiate with the patient (and possibly his family and/or the referring agency) an agreed rationale for his stay on the ward.

"Urgent" problems of this kind do not seem to appear when the reason for admission is agreed upon by the staff, the patient, the family, and the referring agency; all then have the same plan and hopefully are pursuing the same kinds of solution (de Shazer, 1991). Of course, it is typical that these aims are not identical; indeed, this is often the reason for the "problem" in the first place that necessitates a hospital admission.

These "emergencies" tend to occur when any cracks in the plan emerge as the patient turns on the heat and the hierarchical chain of control breaks at its weakest point (Bateson, 1979). What is likely to happen is that either the patient "escapes" or the weight of medical and institutional authority is brought to bear upon the situation in terms of "heavy" medication and Mental Health Law provision. The incongruous hierarchy is thus corrected, and the staff are once again in charge of the timing! In this instance, the third party that forces the decision to be made at ward level is not a police officer, a children's social worker, or a family doctor, as it was in the home example. On this occasion it is the law that demands that a patient should either be free or be put under control; it is a binary digital operation, one that cannot allow for both freedom and control at the same time.

Incidents such as this are seen in different ways according to the platform from which they are viewed, and each sighting is of value. A professor from a university teaching hospital speaking at a case-conference may be able to put the episode into a wider medical perspective than can a nurse at ward level or the patient himself. There is, however, a relationship between the hierarchical level at which problems are defined and the manner in which a medical model is applied. From a more general perspective, a patient is subjected to classification according to how his mental state or behaviour fits in conceptually with that of other groups of patients.

From a standpoint that is closer to the interaction between patient and nurse there is a different way to conceptualize the event: patients in situations such as the one described often wish both to stay and to leave simultaneously. This is not provided for in the legal system, and it is only the medical model that accommodates a person expressing synchronously contradictory behaviour: the patient is described as insane!

If, however, the different viewpoints can be coordinated, then there may be a way of conceptualizing the phenomena that merges the various perspectives into an overall vista—one, moreover, that is more than the sum of its parts, akin to the three-dimensional picture gained from binocular vision (Bateson, 1979).

If the patient who had been called on at home by the doctor, children's officer, and police happened also to be the patient in the ward incident, and if there were a witness to both episodes, then the problem might be formulated in a way that connects the two events. For example, I may talk with a family and their doctor in their home and discover that the pressure to admit a female patient arises from behaviour that indicates that she both wants and does not want to be admitted to the hospital.

This example of working at different levels with respect to the same family problem also illustrates how in a small community there is a possibility of choosing the place from which to define a problem or suggest an action. Normally a hierarchy in an organization is seen as having a structure consisting of fixed positions that are permanently occupied by particular people.

A different model is that of a hierarchy of roles that may be filled by various people who are able to move from one role to another. As a consultant psychiatrist, I am in the role of diagnostician and director of a plan for a patient's overall management. As a family therapist, I sit in the lounge with an extended family, a family friend, and their doctor to address their inability to manage their child effectively or the husband's futile efforts to control his wife. As a doctor "on call" to the ward, I discuss with the nursing staff how best to avoid being forced by the patient to take control of her. Later, as psychodramatist, I might help the patient to work on the abuse she suffered as a child. These different roles enable me to establish a pattern of interventions that connect (Bateson, 1979) with the various crises in the family and on the ward.

This is reminiscent of the psychodrama stage, where the director, the protagonist, and group members change their positions to experience and perceive the situation from different perspectives and vary their roles according to the requirements of the drama. It is the director who provides for himself, with the assent of the group, the autonomy to utilize the spontaneity of the group in finding the appropriate roles to allow the drama to attain its fulfilment.

Through the use of his own role-repertoire as director he summons the group members' participation in enabling the protagonist to develop his own ability to find the required roles for the occasion. The system of role-taking in the psychodrama session becomes self-creative in response to the input of the director's spontaneity, which can be regarded as a source not only of new information but of a new style of interaction.

The play has come full circle. The psychodramatist is again a psychiatrist, but now also one who attempts to adapt his observation point to the area of the problem at hand.

CHAPTER TWO

A psychodrama in action

The psychodrama

The following is a record of a psychodrama undertaken immediately before this chapter was written; it illustrates a number of systemic features of what might be considered a "typical" or random psychodrama. It would be inappropriate to term it "representative", as psychodramas are so difficult to compare, there being no easily recognized standard except in very broad outline. For simplicity, the warm-up is not described in this following narrative (on many occasions, however, its significance for the later phases can be considerable). Psychodramas are best related in the present tense.

SUE

After the group is warmed up, the transition to the action phase takes place with the selection of the protagonist. Sue, aged 28, is chosen, partly because this may be her last session. She has not been a protagonist before; for two weeks she has been giving out strong signals of her ambivalent feelings about "doing" a psychodrama.

This ambivalence, which proves later to be an important feature throughout the psychodrama, is first apparent in the task of deciding whether to volunteer. She says she will be the protagonist if others decide that she "should". In spite of the apparent ambiguity, the director points out that she has actually made the decision (a very important step for Sue), albeit a conditional one. It is, however, unclear whether she would have "decided" without encouragement (possibly expressed or perceived as pressure) from other group members. The significance of this indecisiveness becomes clearer later.

Sue says that there are four issues to work on, and four chairs are taken to represent them (Fig. 2.1): her relationship with her parents, bingeing, cutting her arms, and an episode with her uncle when she was a child. She chooses the first as the most important. A present-day scene is quickly set up.

Her parents (represented by chairs) are facing one another across a table, having a meal. Sue is seated between them, uncomfortable and feeling like a referee. She is then asked to sit in her father's chair and to adopt his role, followed by that of her mother. Finally, in the role of her sister, Jenny, who moved from Guernsey to Germany six years ago, she describes the pattern of family relationships (Fig. 2.2). We learn that Sue has also moved out into a flat within the last year. Two members of the group are chosen to be father and

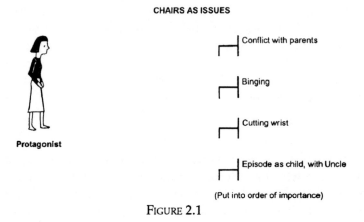

CHAIRS AS ISSUES

Protagonist

Conflict with parents

Binging

Cutting wrist

Episode as child, with Uncle

(Put into order of importance)

FIGURE 2.1

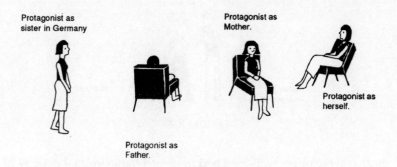

Protagonist as
sister in Germany

Protagonist as
Mother.

Protagonist as
herself.

Protagonist as
Father.

FIGURE 2.2

mother, and the interactions are developed with the help of role-reversals (Fig. 2.3).

Father and Sue enjoy chatting about antiques and ornithology. Mother feels left out of the conversation (she and her husband have few common interests). Father has cooked the main dish. Mother does not take any of the dessert that Sue has prepared, but she asks about the ingredients.

From soliloquies, we learn that father cannot show affection but mother is warm, sociable, and attractive (Fig. 2.4). Father appears to withdraw even more now, as he has learnt that mother has been seeing another man. At first Sue implies that her parents' unhappiness as a couple has resulted from Sue's "psychiatric illness" over the past ten years: mother was so worried about Sue that she sought support and comfort outside the family. Further dialogue, including role reversal, however, shows this not to be the case: father and

Auxiliary
as
Mother.

Protagonist.

Auxiliary
as Father.

FIGURE 2.3

Father is
undemonstrative.   Mother

FIGURE 2.4

mother were never well-matched in regard to the mutual display of affection. Their decision to marry was made under some pressure when father took some leave from an overseas job, fearing that mother was falling for another man. The director reframes Sue's "illness" as something that involved her mother so much that it kept her from missing the affection she never had from father.

Mother is close and shows affection both to Sue and to Jenny. Sue as the daughter still in Guernsey appears to be a "referee": by showing a common interest in antiques with father and by involving mother in her psychiatric problems, she appears to have been "triangulated" by her parents.

At this point the director suggests exploring an earlier issue in order to understand the genesis of the present concern. Sue wants to go back to the matter with her uncle that had begun when she was 8 and continued until she was 15. She mentions a particular occasion when she was 13 years old; she was beginning to develop physically at that age and was feeling extremely uncomfortable about her femininity. The director, who senses that she has a specific scene in mind, suggests that this event be explored.

The scene is a lounge in her home on a Sunday evening. She is sitting on the floor alone. Her family and her uncle's family are in another room. The uncle enters (this is part of a routine that Sue is expecting). He is going to abuse her sexually. Sue allows her uncle to be represented by a black beanbag (having a member of the group as an auxiliary uncle would be too overwhelming for her). As she continues to describe the scene, she becomes so distressed that she is unable to continue in role. Another group member, Jill, is asked to fill the role of 13-year-old Sue (technically, she is termed a "mirror").

This allows Sue some distance from the action, so that she can continue to describe and witness the process. She explains what the uncle starts to do to Sue, that she does not like it, that it hurts her, and he knows that she is upset.

At this point, Sue—with the mirror of Sue (Jill) sitting on the beanbag as though on the uncle's lap—feels unable to continue with the narrative. She feels she is back there at the age of 13, feeling frightened, powerless, and "bad". She exclaims, "I needed 'Sally' to be there." She explains that "Sally" is a person who is now "inside" Sue, but who was not present (or of whom Sue was not aware) when she was 13.

The director does not know Sue very well, but he remembers hearing references being made to her having a multiple personality disorder. He makes a mental note of this and decides to see how Sue employs the character "Sally". He asks Sue to be in the role of "Sally", as though she were there in the scene (Fig. 2.5). "Sally" says that she can be angry: she has cut Sue's arms.

The director suggests that "Sally" speak as a *part* of Sue, if only to allow the psychodrama to be Sue's and not "Sally"'s. This recommendation is also important to maintain a sense of integration and to discourage pathological splitting. With this reframe, Sue is both Sue and "Sally" at the same time and she is able to describe the scene further. When the mirror of Sue (Jill) comes to be lying on the floor, the scene becomes too intense even for Jill, who can no longer sustain the auxiliary role.

The director needs to attend to Jill and take care of her very understandable anxieties. At the same time, it is Sue's psychodrama

Protagonist as "SallY"

Jill as "Mirror" of Protagonist

FIGURE 2.5

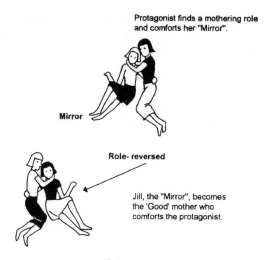

Protagonist finds a mothering role and comforts her "Mirror".

Mirror

Role- reversed

Jill, the "Mirror", becomes the 'Good' mother who comforts the protagonist.

FIGURE 2.6

and not Jill's. Therefore Sue is cast into another role; that of the *caretaker* whom Sue did not have when she was 13. She readily comforts Jill, who is now back in the role of 13-year-old Sue. Asked what figure the comforting Sue feels she is, it appears that she imagines herself to be the mother who was not available to Sue at this time and in this manner.

There follows an important role-reversal: Sue is able at this stage to be the frightened and distressed 13-year-old as she is comforted by the fictitious mother, played by Jill (Fig. 2.6). This time Sue can allow herself to experience the anxieties that had previously been too overwhelming. This is the catharsis of the psychodrama. While being held by the mother-figure, she can express with words and tears her pain and her sorrow. The director explains that she needed this mothering, this "holding" experience, before being ready to express her anger appropriately.

Sue begins to tell her mother (whom she now experiences as if she were indeed her real mother) how she could never discuss this with her when she needed to; her mother had been unable to explain to Sue the meaning of menstrual periods and sex, with the result that Sue was confused by the conversation and jokes of other children at school. In a further role reversal, Sue as mother explains that she, in turn, had not been brought up to find it easy to talk openly about sex.

During this long heart-to-heart talk, Sue also mentions that she has felt "bad and evil". If she touches anyone warmly, she experiences "pain". She says "I am sorry", as if apologizing. The director explains how Sue has unfortunately taken into her self the concept of "badness" that her uncle had pushed on to her until she has come to perceive *herself* as "bad". This is part of what abuse is about— someone like her uncle putting his "badness" into someone else, so that he can feel better.

The director is aware that Sue may well need to talk eventually to her real mother, and that there is information that only she can give. The auxiliary mother (Jill), following a hint from the director, implies that at another time she will speak privately with Sue and will tell her what she needs to know. A transition to the present day is being prepared as a possible prelude to the protagonist being able to talk to her real—as opposed to psychodramatic—parents.

Sue is asked whether she would like a scene in the present day, and she chooses to be with all of her family. The original auxiliary parents (plus one more auxiliary as her sister, Jenny) are called back on to the stage. Sue wants to remain in the middle, but this time to hug them and hold them all together. This she does, and they stand in a close circle for a long time. It is very moving for all of them, and for the group, as she talks of how her life has been affected since her childhood and of how different she wants it to be in the future. She accepts that it feels as if she is now sharing with her real family and that, eventually, she may be able to do so with the actual members of her family in real life.

The psychodrama closes with a considerable amount of warmth, pain, and sadness shared by the other members of the group in relation to their experiences in their auxiliary work and also to what it represented for each of them in terms of their own lives.

Analysis of the psychodrama

Sue's psychodrama will now be analysed according to its constituent themes, in the language of systemic thinking.

(I) *MAP AND TERRITORY*
(STAGED DRAMA—ACTUAL LIFE)

Any description of something is an abstraction, through a process
of coding, of the differences that allow certain salient features to be
defined for recognition by the person to whom the description is
made. In a staged drama, there is an inevitable recursion between
the existential reality of the stage and the actuality of events off-
stage that are being depicted. There is an ambiguity between people
(or objects) regarded as representing other people (or things) off the
stage and those same people or objects experienced as if they really
were those people, and not as simply signifying them.

Sue's parents are represented at times by chairs, at other times by
auxiliaries, and sometimes by Sue herself in role reversal.

This leads to the question of what is meant by an experience of
something as "real". If any "reality" is socially constructed, then
there is no inevitable inconsistency between what is "real" on the
stage and what "really" happened in Sue's parental home.

The reality of the stage and the reality of life off the stage that it
represents are two complementary themes. By making distinctions
between ideas in this way, connections can be made between otherwise separate experiences and phenomena, without blurring the
differences. By maintaining a view that encompasses both complementary themes in a recursive relationship, a splitting into dualities
is avoided, and an epistemological stance that encompasses both
themes is adopted. As the action proceeds, new material becomes
incorporated into the model, and multiple feedback from the director, protagonist, auxiliaries, and other group members facilitates a
refashioning of the themes through the oscillation back and forth of
such complementary opposites as "Stage"–"Life".

From a systems perspective, therefore, the psychodrama can be
discussed in terms of its various complementary themes:

(II) *RECURSIVE COMPLEMENTARITIES*

I refer to the account of first- and second-order cybernetics given by Keeney (1983) and by Keeney and Ross (1985) for a detailed description of the cybernetic concepts employed in this section. I shall use the sign

to indicate a complementary relationship, and

to denote a symmetrical one.

(1)   *Decision–indecision:*
       what constitutes a "decision"?

The question of whether Sue does or does not become the protagonist in the psychodrama is presented to the group. It first appears that she is not making a decision, but she then adds that she would choose to be the protagonist if the group thought she should. From this point of view, she *has* made a decision: to abide by the group's decision! Thus, from

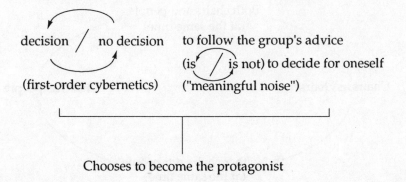

she arrives at the concept that she has "decided", even if this decision is of a different order from a less complicated and unconditional "I will".

(2)   *Chairs–chairs as people:*
      symbolization

The objects do not fully correspond to these people. The chairs signify (1) the idea of the parents or aspects of them and (2) their position vis-à-vis the protagonist and one another—i.e. their relationship. This spatial employment of material symbols to signify ideational concepts or abstract meanings is termed concretization (see chapter one).

The beanbag more vividly represents the uncle's presence, with its blackness signifying a sinister quality.

Beanbag ◄──────────► Beanbag as Uncle

These representations or symbols are not just regarded as objects, nor are they viewed entirely as people; at the very time when they are seen as both people and chairs, they are also felt to be neither just chairs nor whole people. Viewing the totality allows sufficient ambiguity for the two concepts to be played with, not just alternating in time but simultaneously, until the whole recursive process itself represents more than just the constituent aspects. The phenomenon of an ever-changing configuration is well described in the language of gestalt psychology.

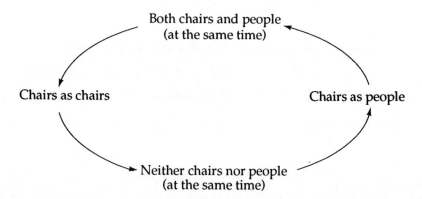

(III) *THE PARTS OF THE SYSTEM ARE INTERRELATED*

(A) *Separateness and connectedness*

Chairs ◄──────────► Issues

The four chairs each represent different issues that Sue wants to work with. The systemic approach involves looking at the connectedness of apparently independent phenomena. Sue sees the issues in order of importance, the most relevant being the first that she mentions. The director suggests that the issues can be linked and that one purpose of the psychodrama is to make the connections visible: her present position with her parents, her eating disorder, her cutting of her arms, and the situation with her uncle will be properly understood only when seen in relation to one another.

(B) *Similarities and differences*

Systems theory is concerned with identifying and comparing the similarities and the differences observed within a given set of phenomena.

(1)   *Perceptions of another person*
(mother as seen from different viewpoints)

Sue's own perception of her mother is compared with how Sue, in the role of her father, sees her mother, and how Sue experiences herself in the role of mother.

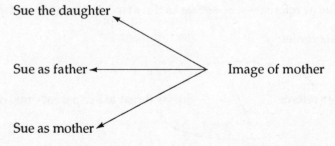

Sue the daughter

Sue as father ◄─────────────► Image of mother

Sue as mother

The three are different: Sue as herself sees mother as feeling excluded from the conversation between Sue and father. Father sees mother as not really wanting him. Mother feels in need of father's affection.

This helps Sue to objectify and externalize the different perceptions of her mother. No single view of mother is the "correct" or only one—they are the different ways in which Sue sees her, and she cannot assimilate these different impressions until she has seen how they are connected with one another. These links are explored by going back in the psychodrama to the history of the parental relationship, where she gains a new impression of how mother's experience of father evolved. In this way Sue's view of mother begins to make more sense; she incorporates father's picture of mother rejecting him for another man with mother's notion of father as always withholding his affection from her.

(2)   *How others appear to perceive oneself* *(how Sue's family appear to view Sue)*

To try to make sense of apparently incompatible phenomena, in the past Sue has attributed the "cause" for these differences to herself— in particular her psychiatric problems, which she supposes her mother has worried about to the extent that she had an affair to find support and consolation.

There is another view that Sue has of herself: that of "referee" or rescuer of her parents' marriage, the person who can interest father in discussion about antiques while showing the warmth to her mother that her father cannot express.

Here, then, is another dichotomy:

Sue as referee ◄——————► Sue as threat to her parents' marriage

This becomes:

Sue as referee   /   Sue as threat to her parents' marriage

Systemic thinking aims both to acknowledge the different perceptions of people and to connect these impressions. Sue, for instance, could simultaneously be both referee and threat: how the roles that Sue actually portrays are defined will depend upon how all three of them (mother, father, and Sue herself) see her.

With regard to the experience and function of social roles, there are some expectations from significant others and some from the subject herself. The better these match, the more there is a sense of coherence (and identity) in the subject's experience of self. These different expectations are regarded as existing in a continual state of flux:

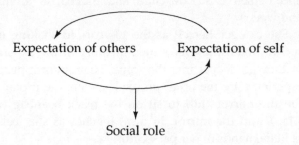

Expectation of others   Expectation of self

Social role

If there is too much rigidity or too wide a fluctuation of expectations in a family setting, there could be some degree of family dysfunction. For an optimal flexibilty of roles, there does need to be a sufficient degree of both consistency and plasticity of expectations.

Furthermore, any shifts in expectations that do occur need to be appropriate and reciprocal. It is one thing for Sue to think of herself as a threat to her parents' marriage, and quite another for her parents to regard Sue as their referee—especially if these opposing attitudes are held at the same time. Such differences are disjointed, cannot be reconciled, and result in an experience of incoherence.

(3)   *The protagonist's own different perceptions of herself*

(a) *Observing self and mirror.* Another example of the differences in perspective gained by assuming various roles is that of Sue in relation to her "mirror"—the role given to Jill. Sue can look at herself as a 13-year-old and see herself more objectively when she is externalized; she can refer to "her" or "she" rather than to "I". This gives her sufficient distance to describe and observe what is happening to the 13-year-old child, what the girl is experiencing, and what she would like to have done about it.

Sue the protagonist ←——————— Mirror of Sue

At the same time, Jill as the mirror is experiencing herself as the subject. She, too, has an image of what is happening in the room. She adopts the posture of the child kneeling upon the floor in fearful anticipation. As she listens to Sue's commentary, she begins to experience herself as Sue the child, and, indeed, she trembles violently and weeps.

Now Sue can see herself as the 13-year-old shaking in terror. This, in turn, intensifies Sue's own memory of the experience, as together they go deeper into the scene. The reinforcement of each one's experience by the other proceeds as Sue the protagonist directs Sue the mirror (Jill) to sit on the black beanbag (now the uncle's lap), and the mirror, in turn, flinches as she feels herself helpless in the hands of her persecutor.

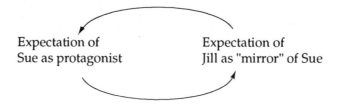

Expectation of
Sue as protagonist

Expectation of
Jill as "mirror" of Sue

This is a cybernetic system of positive feedback, which turns into a "run-away" as Jill, the mirror, herself breaks down in tears when she can no longer contain herself.

There now appears an area of similarity: that of identification. Jill the mirror becomes Jill herself, the group member, responding spontaneously with the feelings that she experiences while in the role of Sue.

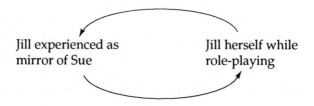

Jill experienced as
mirror of Sue

Jill herself while
role-playing

As she deepens her role, the mirror now gives back messages to the protagonist from herself as Jill . Eventually, when lying on the floor beside the uncle, she involuntarily breaks down, because she, as Jill, can tolerate no more (the director surmises that Jill, too, has had such an experience in her own life; afterwards Jill verifies this).

Now Jill as mirror and Jill as Jill are becoming merged in Jill's experience. As this happens, Sue the protagonist also identifies more closely with her mirror: Sue as her subjective, observing self and Sue as the object become more closely in touch with one another.

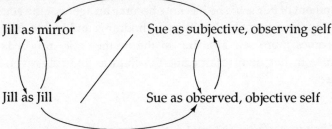

(b) *Subjective self (as a 13-year-old) after role-reversing with mirror.* When Sue has taken the role of the mother-figure that Sue never had and has confronted the mirror of Sue aged 13—played by Jill—the director asks her to become 13-year-old Sue, and Jill to be the "good" mother. This provides Sue with a direct experience of herself as the abused child needing her mother (in this particular psychodrama it would have been too overwhelming to have placed Sue immediately in the action as a subjective 13-year-old).

This process is illustrated diagrammatically below, where the alphabetical letters in inverted commas refer to the roles, and those in the circles signify whether it is the protagonist or the auxiliary who is occupying the role:

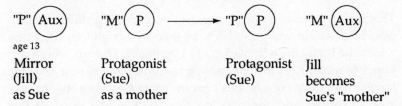

Sue can compare the difference between the situation as it was and the one that should have been. Instead of a mother who is unapproachable about sexual matters, there is a mother who can cope with the subject and support Sue. The role-reversing continues, with the protagonist alternating between her 13-year-old self and the helping mother.

(c) *Subjective self in a newly created role (as a "good mother")*. Another aspect of this role reversal is Sue's own creation of a comforting mother. When Jill breaks down, Sue spontaneously assumes a supportive role, and she develops it further as the role-reversing proceeds. This is not only a new experience for Sue, but also a new development of her self; she has now become an agent of the action. This is a turning-point both in the psychodrama and in Sue. Sue, as she becomes more self-directing in the mother role, proceeds to be so also in her own role of Sue-the-child as the role-reversing continues.

(4)   *How it was/How it might have been*

There is yet another effect of the role reversal at this time. As the difference between the mother as Sue needed her and the mother that she actually remembers becomes more clearly defined, so does the protagonist's understanding. She has a clearer picture of her real mother's difficulty in dealing with sexual topics. No one had instructed mother as a child, and so she, in turn, found it embarrassing to tell Sue about periods, etc. Seeing this aspect of her mother helps Sue to accept her mother's difficulty; Sue begins to think of attempting to talk to her real mother in the present day.

(5)   *How it actually is/How it might be*

This is a step towards the protagonist encountering differences in possibilities. Sue has gone back in time to her childhood, from which she is making a transition to a hypothetical future, where she hopes to mobilize sufficient-enough resources to confront her real family. The difference in this "future projection" is between the kind of contact and conversation that she has had up until the present time, and the one that she will aim to achieve at a later date.

(6)   *A difference becomes a similarity:*
        auxiliary group members "become"
        Sue's real family members

The transition from the past to the future is accomplished by Sue talking with and embracing an "imaginary" family *as if* it were her real family. This is a form of *play* that is not the same as the dramatic and existential experience of the auxiliaries as her *real* family, which comes later. The progression towards the "real" experience is undertaken gradually, to allow the protagonist to find her own way; by attempting to force it, the director could meet with resistance. Thus she embraces the auxiliaries as the auxiliary group *members*, and then, in time, the auxiliaries are reframed by the director as *representing* mother, father, and sister: Sue tells them what happened to her as a child. Finally, while they are embracing, the director raises the possibility that the "mother", "father", and "sister" on the stage essentially do feel like a "real" family. Sue affirms emphatically that they do, indeed. The transition from an experience of interaction with group members, through dramatic fantasy, to an experience of the fantasy as if it were reality, has been made.

Sue, the "family", and the group are profoundly moved as they stand close together, sharing with Sue her experience as she relates her childhood ordeals. She talks of how being touched by anyone was experienced as physical pain.

This final aspect of the psychodrama action is achieved when Sue bridges the difference between a sense of *playing* at being with a family and an experience of *actually being with them*; this change in context from play (or "as if") on the stage to that of an authentic experience of being at her home with her real family has a dream or trance-like quality. This is the dramatic reality.

This is an example of how a systemic approach not only involves seeing phenomena within a context; it can also "mark the context" by altering the punctuation of the narrative. The director, by saying "this is play", establishes the action in the context of play with a certain meaning ("play at playing"). When the director says "this is now your real family in the front lounge", the context is shifted, and it becomes "play at being real people". "Now you really are real people" is yet another re-definition, which, if accepted, transcends the experience of "playing at".

(C) *Bridging dichotomies: seeking fresh connections after defining new differences*

In addition to deriving connections between these main complementary phenomena, the psychodrama addresses (by implication) the following dichotomies by seeking aspects of inter-relatedness after differences have already been defined:

(1)   *Sue and "Sally"*

These are seen by Sue as separate selves; she is asked to portray Sally as a part or aspect of Sue, so that, instead of disclaiming responsibility for cutting herself, she can see that "responsibility" (here a social construct) may not be the entire issue. Factually, Sue cut her own wrists, but she could not see how to cope with the situation in any other way: she does not necessarily have either to own or to disavow "responsibility"! She is able, in this way, however, to accept her agency in the matter.

(2)   *Observing group and identifying (experiencing) group*

The group moves from an observing role at one stage of the action through the mental mechanism of introjective identification to a subjective, experiencing, and empathic role at another—where, for example, in the final family scene many group members are overcome with emotion.

(3)   *Feeling and being*

Sue's perception of herself as "bad" appears to be modified by the group's perception of her as "not bad". She sees another possibility: she may *feel* "bad" and yet not *be* "bad". What was important here was to avoid the "bad/not bad" dichotomy by considering the interrelationship between the feeling of badness and the ascription of badness.

(4)   *The cause and the effect*

Sue's position vis-à-vis her parents' marriage can be seen in two ways: Sue had deduced that the reason for her mother having an affair was that she had sought consolation because she was worried by Sue's illness. The director offers the alternative suggestion that Sue's psychiatric condition has helped mother to fill her empty life: it had taken her mother's mind off an unsatisfactory aspect of their marriage while at the same time keeping her parents together. Sue has also managed to maintain a balance between her parents by sharing with her father a strong mutual interest in antiques.

This reframing of the meaning of Sue's illness does not have to be the whole truth, and, of course, even if it is valid, it is an over-simplification. However, it enables Sue for the first time to see that there are alternative possibilities to Sue's illness as the "cause" of her parents' unhappiness. In systemic terms, there would be neither a "cause–effect" description nor an "either/or" explanation. A cir-cular causality would be evoked, in which Sue's symptoms would have both positive and negative implications for each member of the family. Further psychodramas or family therapy sessions could explore this particular issue. The significance for Sue is that after the psychodrama she ceases to attribute the present unhappiness in her parents' marriage to herself or to something "inside" herself.

(5)   *The self "inside" and the self "outside"*

The notion of an "inside" in contrast to an "outside" is another dichotomy that needed to be bridged. "Inside" Sue feels "bad" and angry, while "outside" she attempts to please others; her voice is muted, and she cannot express anger. Since the anger inside is felt only by Sue, she experiences herself as the object but not the agent or subject of the anger. She feels it to be expressed *against* herself but not as inflicted *by* herself; she invents another self, named "Sally", to externalize the anger when her arms are slashed.

This duality of coexisting selves was resolved by encouraging Sue to think of Sally as a *part* of Sue and not as a separate entity; by role-reversing as Sally, Sue was Sally *as well as* Sue. This broadened the extent of Sue's experience and concept of herself to encompass a "Sally" quality rather than to split it off.

(6)   *Anger and need for love*

Sue's own anger towards others was not addressed in the psychodrama; the anger has to be understood and managed in relation to its opposite, and it was this that was missing in Sue. She could not cope with her own anger, without perhaps feeling that she would disintegrate, until she could experience acceptance and love through the holding by her mother, or those representing her, of her aggressive anxieties, thus containing the feelings that Sue by herself could not manage.

While the connection between being held and the ability to deal with anger were not directly addressed in the psychodrama, it was implied in the switch from the fearsome scene with the uncle to a supportive and comforting encounter between mother and child (the director did, however, mention that this was the first, most fundamental need of the protagonist). Sue afterwards said that right up until this comforting scene, she had experienced being touched by somebody as physical pain (she had possibly projected her own anger onto others, who were then perceived as inflicting it upon herself). At this time, in fact, the auxiliary family were supported, in turn, by the whole group, which provided a more encompassing framework to "be there" for Sue to help to contain her pain and her anxieties about her anger and loss of control.

(7)   *Autonomy and control by others*

Sue ends the psychodrama speaking and relating to others spontaneously, apparently free of external constraint. It is important to try to be sure that she is not responding to pressure from the expectations of the director and the group.

Throughout a psychodrama, decisions need to be made about how the psychodrama itself is to proceed:

- when to pass from description to action;
- when to give space for the protagonist to find his own solution, rather than offer suggestions;
- whether to explore the past, present, or future;

- whether a particular scene is a necessary encounter or an avoidance;
- when to move from one scene to another (one of the most critical decisions).

These choices are often made after negotiation between protagonist and director, with further help from members of the group.

It is in these kinds of deliberations that the issue of autonomy is constantly being attended to. In systemic terms, "pure autonomy" cannot exist, since everything is a part of and is influenced by a larger whole. The psychodrama cannot always go the way of the protagonist (a monodrama is the nearest approximation), because there has to be a context for a psychodrama to be a psychodrama! The group of people who make this context possible are not automatons, and the director should not feel himself to be a "robot". They are not to be viewed as part-objects, but as whole people. They cannot not respond, just as one cannot not communicate. The protagonist will, therefore, discover feedback from the people he encounters during the drama, both on the stage and from the rest of the group.

(IV) *THE DIRECTOR AS AN ORGANIZER OF FEEDBACK (AN OPERATOR OF CYBERNETIC RECURSIVENESS)*

In systemic terms, it is one of the director's main jobs to offer opportunities for feedback to the protagonist and to help the protagonist to be aware of it. Feedback in psychodrama consists of the responses to what the protagonist says or does. When presented with these responses, the protagonist has some knowledge of the effect of his thoughts or actions upon others and, in turn, cannot be unaffected by this. Autonomy is not an absolute that implies that one either does or does not have it. Nevertheless, a greater degree of autonomy is usually what is sought for, especially where there is a sense of rigidity or of being too much under control, whether of self or of others.

The question for the director, therefore, is how to help the protagonist to elicit and interpret feedback. With those protagonists who are set in their attitudes and patterns of behaviour, the more this information is available, the more alternative options and choices the protagonist may have, and the greater his sense of autonomy—with one important proviso: that the protagonist feels able to exercise these choices.

(V) *CHANGE: CORRELATIONS OF BELIEF, PERCEPTION, AND ACTION*

Fundamental to a systems view of change is the inter-relatedness of meaning (or belief), perception (according to the viewpoint), and events (action/behaviour). The connection between behaviour and perception can be described in terms of a recursive process betwen an act and the information resulting from it: a cybernetic unit in which feedback influences the original behaviour.

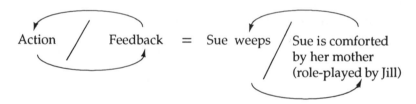

It is a breakthrough for Sue to cry with anyone, and the comfort from the complementary parental role is the positive feedback that enhances this.

There is another aspect to this, which concerns the particular perception that the protagonist has of the feedback he or she receives: what the protagonist notices may not be what the director or group members observe, and so their respective interpretations of what they see may be different. For example, Sue pronounces herself to be responsible for what happened with her uncle, whereas the group members view her as a frightened, confused, and helpless victim.

It is an awareness of these differences in perception, made possible by these psychodramatic techniques, that affords the protagonist an opportunity to look at his perceptions in a different light, and to see that there are other possible ways of apprehending phenomena. Here, again, are more options for freeing a protagonist from too restrictive a vision. Eventually, the protagonist becomes influenced not only by the perceptions, but also by the evaluations of these other group members as expressed through their behaviour (action/words). Thus, one recursive cycle:

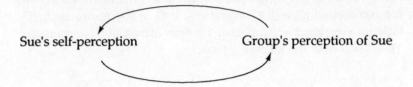

Sue's self-perception   Group's perception of Sue

turns into another:

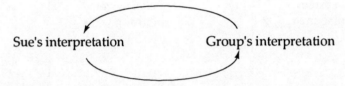

Sue's interpretation   Group's interpretation

Differences in perception and belief are themselves part of a recursive process:

Belief   Perception

Sue feels "pain" if she is physically touched by someone—an indication to her that she is "bad", which is another example of a positive, reinforcing feedback:

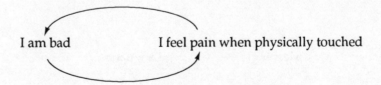

I am bad   I feel pain when physically touched

This pattern is broken during the psychodrama by the interplay between the other recursive processes, and it becomes:

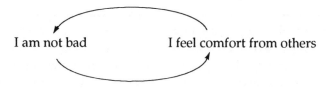

I am not bad   I feel comfort from others

These recursive processes indicate that in psychodrama the inter-change between perception, action, and belief reaches a stage when the belief systems of the protagonist and of the group mutually influence one another, until they become shared, even if indirectly. This is shown in the following loop:

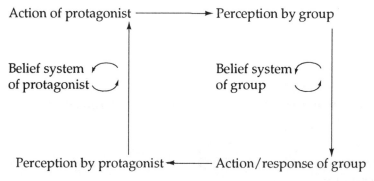

Action of protagonist ⟶ Perception by group

Belief system of protagonist

Belief system of group

Perception by protagonist ⟵ Action/response of group

One final aspect of this interplay needs consideration—namely, that psychodrama, like other therapies, uses the medium of lan-guage. Change is influenced by the different meanings that become attached to sequences of behaviour, according to how the context is understood. Meanings are organized through conversation and dia-logue (Anderson, in press). It is through the establishment over time of a common language that a consensus of meaning is reached between protagonist, director, and group members as they struggle with what, for example, is meant by "bad" in this particular context of psychodrama and language.

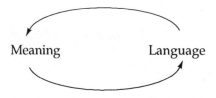

Meaning   Language

The psychodramatic exploration of transgenerational psychiatry: "sins of the fathers"

I n this chapter I illustrate the way psychodrama can be applied to a particular conceptual model of family systems theory, rather than to systemic therapy in the more general sense, as used in the Milan approach. The "multi-generation transmission process" as expounded by Bowen (1978) conceives family dysfunction as arising from the operation of a family's emotional system over several generations.

Much family therapy involves working with family-of-origin issues and some practitioners consider these to be the most fundamental concerns. Bowen (1978) originated this field of study which has been developed by his followers, including Guerin (1976) and Fogarty (1978). Framo (1982) brought object relations theory to bear on the subject, and Boszormenyi-Nagy (1981) introduced the concept of a ledger of ethical obligations extending across generations. Lieberman (1979) in England and Roberto (1992) in the United States have reviewed transgenerational theories and therapies. These clinicians and many others have emphasized the importance of patients addressing these topics directly with the family members concerned wherever this is possible.

Working with families-of-origin, when it is practically possible, is rewarding but often challenging for the very reasons that make it necessary: relatives are frightened of encountering one another with matters that they believe will result in deep distress. They can keep information and feelings about one another secret all their lives. Historical facts, hidden alliances, resentments concerning unfulfilled obligations, feelings of everlasting indebtedness, split loyalties, the hurt of old wounds, or the pain of past disappointments may all linger and fester indefinitely, even though they may be outside the awareness of the people most concerned.

Sometimes the distress—and often the attendant anger—is so unacceptable, even to the person carrying it, that he breaks off all contact with his relatives and represses all thoughts and feelings about some, or all, of his family members. This "emotional cut-off" was described by Bowen, who discovered its profound importance, both for the person who "cuts off" and for the family who are disowned. The deep effect upon the subject who "cuts off" is not self-evident; it often comes to light only when the unacknowledged consequences of these "cut-offs" are felt in his own new family.

The remaining family that has been thus disconnected has also lost a part of itself that it may not have the opportunity to restore and to integrate. Indeed, sometimes it is the main body of the family that "disowns" one of its members in an effort to rid itself of unacceptable pain or seemingly unresolvable conflict.

Such issues are usually never confronted, either by the individual in private or by the family members collectively; the "unfinished business" is taken to the grave.

Ideally, when a therapist finds evidence of these intergenerational issues he can encourage the family to bring the members of the extended family into the therapy sessions. This may, however, not always be practicable, and family members may refuse to attend. Even so, much helpful work can be accomplished by coaching (Bowen, 1978) people on how to approach uncooperative family members and how to engage them in dialogue over delicate issues. Writing letters to those far afield (as emotionally "cut-off" people often are) can be very helpful.

Often, however, the other people concerned are dead or untraceable. It is here that psychodrama is particularly effective in helping to investigate the origins of their dysfunction by finding out

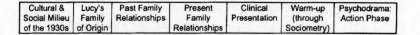

Cultural & Social Milieu of the 1930s	Lucy's Family of Origin	Past Family Relationships	Present Family Relationships	Clinical Presentation	Warm-up (through Sociometry)	Psychodrama: Action Phase

SYSTEMIC PROCESSING: RETROSPECTIVE ISOMORPHISM

THE CONTEXT OF THE CONTEXT.

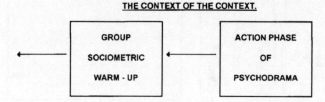

FIGURE 3.1

what they already "know" (but do not know they know!) and piecing together the threads and connections between the living and the dead. Unfinished business can be undertaken when the dead are brought psychodramatically to life.

This chapter is presented, like a family-of-origin issue, in a reverse sequence of time (Fig. 3.1), to illustrate the kind of thinking required to pass from a presenting problem to its origin in previous generations. The type of question—such as "how did this person come to be here today in this way with this particular difficulty?"— is addressed by starting with an account of a patient and her psychodrama and then asking, "how did she ever come to this group that participates in psychodrama, and how did she get to do this specific psychodrama on this particular day with this group of people with their own various agendas?" We begin, therefore, with the action phase of the psychodrama and then examine the warm-up and the means of selection of the protagonist. The process of working backwards in time will help us to understand transmission of dysfunction down the generations by the family of the protagonist.

LUCY

Lucy, a lady of 61 who had never in her life seemed to have been a happy person, appeared to make a significant response to just one psychodrama. For years she had suffered a fear of being alone, combined with being afraid to go outside her home.

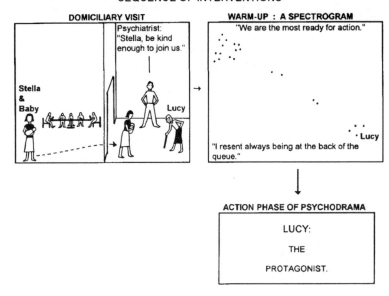

FIGURE 3.2

Her marriage had finished fifteen years earlier. She had been living on her own, with the solitude broken by daily visits from her married daughter, Stella; but the latter was no longer able to make the journey, having just given birth to her fourth baby.

Lucy had severe heart disease which made it difficult for her to stand or to walk more than a few steps at a time. She had recently moved in with her daughter, but this had not worked out: they were a large three-generation family occupying a flat with three bedrooms. A domiciliary visit (Fig. 3.2) by the director had revealed the problem. The daughter and her family did not want to be involved in any contact with the social services. (A reading of the local press clarified this: Lucy's ex-husband had been detained for questioning in connection with an alleged case of indecent assault.) There was evidently a fear that the family was going to be invaded by officials inquiring into the safety and well-being of the extended family.

The home situation was fraught and chaotic. Stella and her mother were not talking to each other. The director managed to establish a dialogue between them to find out what this was about.

The problem needed to be approached on two complementary fronts: the housing situation and the family relationships. It was decided to offer day treatment and to help with the housing at the same time.

Lucy attended the day programme with great apprehension and serious misgivings. She was very frightened that her daughter would be upset at the thought of being talked about. The atmosphere at home was taking its toll on Lucy, who had to spend most of her time in the same room as her daughter, with no mediator. Lucy appeared worried, afraid, dejected, and defeated.

In the warm-up of her psychodrama, Lucy had spoken of being angry with two people, but of being unable to express it.

Lucy's psychodrama: the action phase

Lucy begins the psychodrama by saying that these two people (Fig. 3.3) are her ex-husband and her eldest daughter, Stella.

The first scene, in the present day, depicts Lucy with Stella in their home. Stella does not do much housework, in spite of having four children. In the role of her daughter, Lucy explains that there is no point in tidying up, as the children would reduce the room to a state of chaos again within minutes. Her attention is taken up almost entirely by her baby. With Stella's role taken by an auxiliary group member, Lucy asks whether she can clean the kitchen floor; role-reversing with the daughter, Lucy as Stella forbids her to help. Back in the role of the protagonist, Lucy declares that she feels "terrible and useless".

From Lucy in the role of Stella we hear that the daughter claims to have invited her mother to live with her out of concern for Lucy's loneliness. She then adds that she is worried lest "other people" might think that her mother had been taken into the home to be made use of as a housemaid. She happens to mention that the expected housing grant and attendance allowance has not materialized, thus leaving Stella without financial assistance. There appears to be an unstated and perhaps unintended implication that Stella might be protesting her unselfishness too much, and that her motives are more complex.

FIGURE 3.3

Further role reversal ends with Lucy in the role of her daughter, expressing in soliloquy her resentment of her mother and her wish to take revenge for the way mother "used" Stella when she was a teenager.

(No one may know Stella's true motives—not even, perhaps, Stella. This is Lucy's sense of Stella's feelings, which she gains through interaction with the auxiliary and by role reversal.)

FIGURE 3.3 *(continued)*

The next scene, therefore, is set twenty years ago, in Lucy's family home, when Stella is 16, the oldest of five children with the task of providing company for her agoraphobic mother. She is kept back from school, helps with the housework, and acts as her mother's "lifeline" by visiting the shops. In the role of 16-year-old Stella, Lucy reports that, far from resenting her position, Stella enjoys it: it gives her a sense of power over her mother.

Lucy then refers to her husband—a taxi driver—who is almost always out of the home, returning in the early hours. Lucy stays up for him with a cooked meal, but he is always drunk and physically abusive to her. With the bruises he inflicts, she is afraid to go out in case they are noticed. She feels humiliated to know that the neighbours can hear the noise of her husband's angry outbursts.

The director wonders what it was about Lucy, even twenty years ago, that allowed her to be prepared to suffer humiliation. Was it purely that neither she nor anyone else could have done anything about such a situation, or was there also something about Lucy herself that she endured it? The systems view would be that the marital relationship and Lucy's personality were each a part of a more extensive and recurring pattern, which has been described as a "trauma-organized system" (Bentovim, 1992). There was a sense of reproach and martyrdom emanating from Lucy as she reported her life story.

Lucy is asked by the director where her feeling of powerlessness originated. How did it come about that she has never appeared to allow herself the relief and satisfaction of expressing anger? She explains that she has always felt powerless: "I was an illegitimate child in the 1930s, and I lived with my grandparents. I thought they were my parents, and that my aunts were my sisters. My real mother handed me to my grandmother when I was five months old, and was later evacuated during the war. My grandfather had died and there were no men in my life when I was a child."

Lucy reports that she was only given this information when she was 12; she had not shown any striking reaction to this news, and she thinks that she might already have sensed that something in her family relationships was not quite straightforward. At this time the matter of her real father had not been raised, nor was it explained why her mother had "given" her to her grandmother.

Lucy goes on to explain that when she was 16 (Stella's age in the previous scene!), she had heard her relatives mention what she had taken to be her real father's name; they appeared not to have realized that Lucy was present, and there was an embarrassed silence as her relatives glanced at Lucy. Lucy could not do much with this information, as she had not had the "courage" to confront her grandmother.

The psychodrama continues with a scene in which Lucy is asked to achieve what she had been unable to accomplish at the time: an encounter that had never occurred, but which should have taken place.

With an auxiliary in the role of her grandmother, Lucy asks pointedly about her father and her background. Why had she never been told about this? Why was it left for her to find out?

After reversing roles with her grandmother, the protagonist explains that it was feared that Lucy might have "leaked" the information to outsiders: her real father was from a well-known, prominent family, who knew nothing of Lucy's existence. News could get back to them. Her true father is married. Lucy's mother was a servant in their house. Furthermore, the grandmother was resentful of her daughter's conduct and of the shame brought upon the family.

As the role reversal between Lucy and her grandmother proceeds, Lucy oscillates between the roles of the 16-year-old and the adult present-day Lucy. (This scene is not a past event that *could* have happened. As a teenager, she would not have been able to formulate the questions; Lucy needs to be in a different role to confront her grandmother. This, therefore, is more like the present-day, adult Lucy, bringing her grandmother back to life so that she can pick some bones with her.)

As the dialogue continues, Lucy discerns that her grandmother and her family have been protecting themselves from being figures of shame in the community and covering up for the father and his family. It was as if the reputation of the father's family was more important than their own feelings; the "shame" was regarded as belonging entirely to Lucy's mother, and none of it to the father.

As an example of the class system as it was in the first half of the century, the conversation shows how in this community the boundaries between social classes were exceptionally firmly drawn. In matters of conflict between the classes, the poor were inclined to be regarded (even by themselves) as being "in the wrong", and the rich as "upright". The gender roles were equally distinct: the woman who became pregnant from an extra-marital liaison frequently had to "carry the can", while the man's behaviour could be overlooked.

For Lucy, there was yet another indignity: the young were held to be accountable to their elders and to be in their sway. Respect was due towards the older generation, and consideration for the elders was paramount, even to the detriment of the young. She was not trusted to keep a family secret (which involved herself, perhaps, more than anyone else), and she was not given the honour of being told her own father's name. Furthermore, such was the disregard of any such considerations that Lucy did not feel authorized even to ask. Hardly, therefore, was it befitting for her to express her indignation over her enforced ignorance.

Such attitudes of adults can be so pervasive with children that they may not even conceive of an alternative: Lucy had incorporated the values that had been inculcated, without it ever being acknowledged that they were thus instilled. This insidious subjugation of her mind could not have been resisted at the time, because she was unaware that it was happening. This, in the language of psychological defence mechanisms and object-relations theory, was an "introjection" of the suppresser. Lucy could not conceive of trust and respect from her elders and "betters".

Thus Lucy, through the role-playing interaction between herself (at 16 and as an adult) and her grandmother, comes to the realization for the first time that her lowly attitude to herself (which has profoundly affected her disposition towards others) developed when she assimilated the image that her grandmother and family had of themselves, of her real mother, and of herself. It appears that Lucy had come to represent her mother and to epitomize the family's ignominy. She had become a scapegoat for her family, regarding herself as the object of shame that her family had assigned to her (Bollas, 1987).

In the psychodrama, she has found a new role as a 16-year-old berating her grandmother for keeping her ignorant. She demands to know the facts, protesting her claim to be acknowledged in her own right (exemplified by being told her own father's name) and to be recognized as having a place with some roots in a society rather than to be hidden away as a pariah.

Lucy, following these insights, next declares, "I can see the same thing happening with my daughter and one of my grandchildren"—the identical process is being transmitted to further generations.

Near the end of the psychodrama, in the role of her grandmother, the protagonist declares that she, the grandmother, is actually very fond of Lucy: the problem is that she is unable to explain or to express what she feels. In other words, there is an important distinction between the figure that Lucy represents and the feelings that her grandmother has towards her as her adopted child—sentiments that are perhaps prevented from being expressed, insofar as Lucy cannot be unequivocally acknowledged as a person in her own right. It is also possible that the grandmother does not feel she should treat Lucy as her own child. Keeping the secret means that grandmother can neither explain that Lucy is not her own natural child, nor maintain a convincing pretence that she is.

Seemingly, grandmother also has a low sense of self-esteem and thus finds it difficult to declare her own warmth and regard for those she loves. In this psychodramatic enactment, however, the protagonist, in the role of her grandmother, is able to embrace the auxiliary portraying Lucy; back in the role of Lucy, the protagonist is, in turn, given a warm hug by her grandmother. The protagonist, through the admission of what *should* have happened from the experience of how it *might* have come to pass, has come to the acceptance of what in actuality did not take place.

In the sharing stage of the psychodrama, the subject centres upon the sense of pride that some group members feel they lost when they became fatherless. Fathers seem to have defined the position of children in the patriarchal society of those pre-war years.

Lucy was transformed after the psychodrama. The down-trodden "doom-and-gloom" appearance lifted. She was appreciative of the company and gave of herself, both within therapy groups and outside them. A little later Lucy was given half-way house accommodation as an interim measure, and since then she has found a new home.

This is a psychodrama that displays two significant features, which, while recognized as commonly applying to psychodramas in general, are especially clearly shown here. The first is the degree of archaeological self-inquiry (Epston & White, 1990) required to recover the start of a life script or "narrative" in order to transform it. Lucy herself provides almost all the "input": she extracts information from her own memory system, sorts it, and organizes it to make a meaningful history. If there were no auxiliaries, it would be termed a monodrama. However, she makes good use of them, if only as embodiments of her own experience of people: the auxiliaries behave as Lucy asks them to, and they do not have to provide information of their own. In other words, this is like a play-back of Lucy's internalized past, to allow her to separate and arrange the various ingredients before finally editing them and re-writing the faulty script.

The second distinctive feature is its implication for the relationship between Lucy and the group. While it is a revelation to herself as she explores her past, the dramatization is also a matter of Lucy laying herself bare to the members of the group. This has significance for Lucy as a kind of "rite of passage" (Kobak & Waters, 1984) into the group—as if replacing the absence of any formal initiation into adulthood in her own life. This psychodrama is like a ceremony, with Lucy, her origins having been acknowledged, henceforth becoming accepted as part of the wider community.

Lucy's warm-up (Fig. 3.2)

The warm-up had a sociometric quality (for one of his classical expositions of sociometry, I refer the reader to Moreno, 1937b, and for a recent full account of the sociometric implications of psychodrama, I recommend Williams, 1991). There were newcomers to the group. People were asked to identify those they did not know, and then to assess from non-verbal body language those whom they considered to be the most "warmed-up"—that is, feeling spontaneous and ready to participate. They were also asked to verify their hunches by checking their perceptions with the people concerned in order to correct any projections or other inaccurate observations.

A spectrogram was then formed by the group members standing along a line that indicated the degree of spontaneity or energy of each member. At the "hottest" end were two clusters: they were asked to discover what was different about them as individuals that they were bunched into two gatherings rather than into just one. This resulted in a further split into four smaller sub-groups.

At the opposite end of the spectrogram were four people, including Lucy. They were asked to split into two sub-groups and to discuss, with the group listening, how they were to do this. They inquired among themselves what was actually meant by being "warmed-up". What was the real meaning of this criterion? They decided that the least "warmed-up" were those most anxious and uncomfortable: Lucy and another group member.

These two were asked if they would like to move to another part of the group, where they would feel more comfortable than at the end of the spectrogram. Lucy found a different spot.

During these negotiations, Lucy had first gone to what might have been regarded as the "back of the queue". She then stated that she felt resentment but was unable to express this, because when she spoke the group responded with a long silence (this was, indeed, correct). When allowed to move, she chose to sit in the centre of the group and spoke in more depth about her bitterness.

Some other members of the group then voiced objections to their being instructed to form themselves into sub-groups and asked the director why he had suggested this. His reply was that some group members had been finding it difficult to form their own *functional* sub-groups and were therefore likely to find themselves placed by others into sub-groups more according to *stereotypes* —that is, how they were seen rather than how they really were.

There was a further silence, which was broken by Lucy speaking yet again of her resentment. She was clearly ready to enlarge upon this. One of the nursing staff suggested that Lucy be the protagonist, and the rest of the group began to accede to this idea.

During the psychodrama itself, the implications of the warm-up for the action phase had not been appreciated, but on reflection certain aspects of the warm-up clearly seemed to have a bearing on the action that followed:

1. The group began with the theme of acknowledging those with whom the members of the group had not yet made their acquaintance.

2. People were judged as to their spontaneity and readiness for action by subjective impression, but this was then verified with the members themselves, in order to avoid misapprehension; in other words, people were asked for their own assessments of themselves and not put into categories according to unsubstantiated assumptions.

3. The spectrogram gave each of the group members a choice as to where to place themselves. Some saw this as a manipulation, whereas it was intended to break down the placement of people according to stereotyped notions and to encourage individuals to form their own functional sub-groups (Agazarian, 1993).

4. Lucy had placed herself (but by the same token had also been

placed by the rest of the group) at the "bottom end" of the spectrogram.

5. Lucy utilized an opportunity, while negotiating her place at the bottom end of the spectrogram, to mention her resentment and to voice her disinclination to express her rancour because of the lack of response from the other members of the group.

6. Lucy was given a second opportunity to find her own appropriate place in the group, where she would be comfortable.

7. When allowed after negotiation to find her own position in the spectrogram by her own free choice, she became more articulate and "warmed-up"

In retrospect, this warm-up appeared to be an enactment that was a microcosm of three aspects of Lucy's life story: (1) her personal history; (2) her arrival at the day unit; and (3) her own psychodrama, which had begun with her feeling as if passively placed at the end of the line (spectrogram) but ended with her actively taking steps to reassert her position. The director could have represented the father she had never had, who gave her a "place" in the group community!

SUMMARY

Telfner (1991) points out that in systems terms what is more complex can explain what is simpler.

This chapter has been about working backwards and placing presenting material into a gradually wider context as the process continues (Fig. 3.1). The action of the psychodrama was this same procedure in microcosm. It began with Lucy's impossible situation in her daughter's home, and their inability to communicate. She was referred to the author (who was her psychiatrist as well as the director of the psychodrama) by a housing association, because she had no home to go to and did not seem to "belong" anywhere. It continued with an exploration of the resentment of the daughter, Stella, of her position with regard to her mother twenty years previously, when Stella was aged 16. At that time, Lucy was an underfunctioning mother with an unhappy marriage.

The action went on to explore the origin of Lucy's sense of powerlessness and low social status that arose from the position of her own mother, her relationship with her grandmother, and, above all, the withholding of all knowledge about her father.

The warm-up had explored the status of the group members with regard to one another, to the group as a whole, and to the director. This process allowed attention to be focused upon Lucy's resentment at being "at the bottom of the line", which, in turn, had been revealed when the sociometric and functional sub-grouping divided the personal issue from the stereotype (Agazarian, 1993). That process itself had arisen from the fact that at the beginning of the session there were newcomers who had needed to find out where they "fitted in" with the rest of the group.

Thus the theme of where new people stand in relation to the group that they enter is similar to that of the psychodrama action, where Lucy was struggling to find out her position as a youngster (and, indeed, where she was as a baby) in relation to her relatives.

This isomorphism (Bateson, 1979) is displayed even further back in the preliminary contact that the director had with Lucy in her daughter's home (Fig. 3.2), where the daughter was in charge and Lucy appeared a "useless" burden, taken into the home on mistaken assumptions or for dubious intentions.

Lastly, the whole pattern of events was taking place while Lucy's ex-husband was under investigation for a possible charge of indecent assault—a situation in which, ironically, in order for justice to be done, the family had to endure the fear of the social disgrace of the publicity.

The whole psychodrama session turned the position on its head. Lucy became the "chosen one" and was incorporated into the group in her own right and with respect.

CHAPTER FOUR

Strategic psychodrama: helping an abusive mother to converse with her children's social worker

"Strategic psychodrama" is a term used by Williams (1989) to emphasize psychodrama's pragmatic, problem-solving functions, as distinct from the aesthetic, self-revelatory, and cathartic qualities derived from its theatricality. I use the term to denote a psychodrama undertaken with a specific goal in mind, over and above the more general aims of releasing a patient's spontaneity, developing insight, gaining a greater sense of self, or acquiring new roles. The following psychodrama was carried out with the intention of moving towards a particular objective in the overall management plan of a patient.

DAWN

Dawn had reached an impasse in her dealings with a social worker who had had to remove Dawn's second baby into care after alleged physical mistreatment. Dawn had been devastated, but the social worker had felt that there was no choice: she had given Dawn a great deal of support over some years, especially when Dawn's first child was fostered. It appeared that Dawn had come to regard the social worker, Ruth, as her only confidant, and she had felt bitterly betrayed, refusing all further contact.

Efforts were being made to help Dawn regain the trusting relationship with Ruth, so that some discussions could take place about future commitments between Dawn and her baby. Dawn, however, had regressed to the developmental phase of a stubborn, defiant, sulking toddler. The baby seemed to have been regarded by this single, isolated mother as all that she had left in the world. (It is just possible that Dawn's regression was a form of identification with her lost child.)

On the afternoon following the morning's psychodrama, Dawn was due to speak to her own nurse key-worker, Donald, with a view to his acting as an intermediary in the forthcoming meeting with Ruth. Dawn had maintained that she could not bring herself to speak with Ruth. Arrangements, however, needed to be made for the long-term care of the baby: the future relationship between Dawn and her baby was hanging in the balance.

The warm-up

Dawn's psychiatrist, who is directing the psychodrama session, has no preconceived plan for Dawn to be the protagonist; she would be the least likely person in the group to volunteer, or even to be persuaded.

The "warm-up" process puts Dawn's psychodrama into context: what kind of psychodrama is done often depends upon how the protagonist is selected, and this, in turn, has a great deal to do with the climate of the group in the session and what individual or group concerns the members have brought in with them.

The director tries, in the warm-up, to clarify these issues to enable the group as a whole and the future protagonist to understand, later in the session, the connection between the form of the action phase and their own agendas (Williams, 1991). He asks the group members whether, and in what way, the group feels different from the previous session a week earlier (there are some empty chairs in the circle). One patient remarks that there is a nurse from the acute admission ward visiting the group for the session. Another patient reports that there are "less people" today. The director tries to find out how each person sees the differences from the previous week.

He then asks how members *feel* about these differences: what is it like to have a smaller group? Reference is made to the empty chairs. Liz remarks that she is on a high chair, so that she does not fall asleep. Peter prefers a bigger group, because he can hide in the crowd. Amanda says that a large group is less preferable, since people do not speak; Liz feels that large groups are claustrophobic.

The director asks a reflexive (Tomm, 1987) question, using a hypothesized change of context: "What if there is a group of only five people, and still nobody speaks?" "We would always speak in such a small group", they all reply.

The director remarks that the various ways in which group members are affected by different aspects of the group, such as its size, reflect differences within the group members themselves.

After a pause, the group members are asked what is now needed to enable the group to proceed. Amanda replies that the group needs to be motivated. *How* to become motivated is the next question, but it baffles the group members. The director then changes the mode of relating from "thinking" to "doing": this is, after all a "warm-up"! "Let us *do* something different!" he importunes. "Let us get up from our chairs and, in any way we wish, involve ourselves with one another without talking. We might walk around the room, or we might stand still . . .". All except Vincent stand up and walk.

Some look at each other, but many avoid eye contact. One or two touch an arm of another. Two women give each other a hug and then involve Dawn in their embrace, as if they are a family. Vincent stands still; he is not going to be "like a flock of sheep".

The director then suggests that they should also talk. Some sit down in pairs or in small groups. Those still standing or walking feel as if those sitting down are "observing" them. The director suggests that one of those standing, Amanda, might like to think of a way to find out whether this is so.

Vincent then begins a discussion about staff (he was already very angry with them from the previous day). Staff (who, also, are "observers") are not "on the line". They don't have to be apprehensive, like other group members, for they will not be protagonists. "Yes", replies the director, "we are, indeed, privileged!" This remark hurts Vincent, who later declares that it would be helpful to see a psychodrama with "normal" people as protagonists. Cathy, one of the nurses, maintains that she feels emotionally involved with protagonists and wants their psychodramas to go well. The director points out that staff frequently act as auxiliaries.

In systemic terms, the group is exploring the differences between staff and patients.

A further point of discussion concerns the director's style of conducting the warm-up: is he organizing the situation or is he not? Is he pretending to take charge when he is not, or is he purporting not to control when in a subtle way he is doing just that? He apparently wishes to know what the group members who are sitting down are feeling; however, instead of directly asking them himself he asks someone else to enquire from a third person whether they can think of a way of finding out the feelings of those who are seated! This is termed a triadic question, a systemic mode of inquiry, and, furthermore, it has been posed as a "meta-question"—that is, not "what are they feeling?" nor "can you find out what they are feeling?" nor even "how can you find out?", but "can you suggest someone who could find a way of finding out?" This, like circular questioning (Penn, 1983), is a way of addressing the interconnections between the thoughts, feelings, and actions of group members as a whole, rather than the director himself simply asking direct questions of individuals or of the group collectively. Such questioning makes the group members more aware of how they link up with one another. It also enables the members to participate actively in their own self-inquiry.

This method of inquiry leads to Amanda stating that she finds it difficult to initiate any conversation—except when she asks a question. When she does this, however, she is very persevering and thorough! From the conversation that follows, it transpires that "sitting" means "tired", "avoiding", or "protesting"—and sometimes all three at once.

The director asks, "Who will be the last person left standing?" This has the obvious effect of the other members quickly sitting down—all except the director himself and Amanda. There is a long pause, as though the group is "stuck" again: has all this been a waste of time? Attention becomes focused upon Katie, a patient who has been giving out very clear signals that she has no intention of becoming involved with whatever is happening in the group. The director remarks that she presents as a bored spectator who is challenging the group to interest her, and that he does not feel like "putting on a show" for her benefit. Katie, even so, gets "feedback" from other group members, since she cannot avoid listening to the discussion about her. Her motivations for attending psychodrama are questioned. She appears solemn and passively hostile. Is Katie expressing the feelings of others in the group? Is unacknowledged and unexpressed anger an issue? Is it directed towards the staff, as Vincent has perhaps implied?

Lynn then tries to break the impasse by suggesting that Judith be the protagonist. Discussion follows: would Judith be doing her work primarily for Judith, with the group then becoming identified and involved in her task, or would Judith be working as the protagonist mainly on behalf of Lynn and some of the members of the group to get them "off the hook", thus enabling some of the members to opt out of their involvement in the group? Judith then announces that she is pregnant, and that a week ago she began to have contractions. There is discussion as to who would be responsible if she miscarries. Some say it would be Judith. Others believe all present would have a joint responsibility. Vincent insists that the director (a doctor) would have the entire responsibility, and that he, Vincent, would not want to be a part of any of it.

Thus the issue is transformed into that of the group's ambivalence over its responsibility. Even to start a discussion or a task requires *someone* to take the first initiative! Is the anger towards the staff an expression of the group's frustration with them for not taking more of the onus? The director remarks that it might first need just a few people to be involved with one another before others could become engaged. However, even for the original "few" to be formed, there may be a need for one person to be the initiator. Is this to be the director? Is this also now an issue of authority? Cathy, one of the nursing staff, is impatient to start; we are wasting time.

It is noticed that Dawn, who is seated next to the director, appears to have fallen asleep. People begin to express indignation, and some insulting remarks are made. It emerges that a very similar episode had occurred the previous week and that Dawn was insulted and "got at" to a considerable degree, especially by Lynn, Vincent, and Judith!

The director comes to the conclusion that some of the hostility towards himself and other staff is on account of their apparent inability to handle Dawn. She has made other group members very frustrated and yet seems not to respond to any expression of their annoyance. Clearly Dawn's "sleeping" is highly provocative. She needs some help, but she is hardly likely to ask for it, let alone agree to any suggestions.

The action

The director wonders whether her "non-voting" with her feet can be reframed as her own way of putting in a bid for some kind of attention. He makes the extremely unusual suggestion that Dawn be the protagonist, despite her not appearing to want it. The group members gather around Dawn, who is still sitting in her chair. Fortunately, the very people who were most critical of Dawn are also those most concerned to help her. They and the director already know that Dawn is to see the nurse key-worker, Donald, in the afternoon to discuss seeing the children's social worker, Ruth, who is negotiating the possibility of Dawn visiting her baby, who has been taken into care. Dawn has been terrified of meeting the children's social worker in case she "blows" the interview and does not get access to her baby, Suzanne. Also, she is feeling very guilty at having failed Ruth, who has given Dawn enormous support over the years.

The action begins with Vincent as the nurse key-worker calling on her at home. To empower him, he is allowed to direct the scene as well as to be one of the principal characters. He comments upon how he is feeling in the part of the key-worker, a role he carries out extremely well. At one point it seems to become Vincent's psychodrama, but later, like a true director, he turns to the group members to ask for their opinion and advice.

Someone is now required to be Ruth, the children's social worker. Lynn offers, having already known something of the proposed meeting with the social worker. Amanda acts as Dawn's double. At this point Dawn, who has continued to remain slumped in her chair, begins to take more notice. She finally agrees to reverse roles with Ruth, and she clarifies the purpose of the interview.

In the role of Ruth, she explains that Dawn had been married to Brian—someone she had been close to from a very early age, as they had lived just a few doors away from one another. Brian's mother had frequently taken Dawn into her own home because Dawn's mother had not found it easy to cope with her, even as a young child. Brian had initially been like a sort of foster-brother. Their marital relationship was severely strained when a (male) drug dealer from England arrived on the scene. Eventually Brian and Dawn were separated, and their son was taken into care.

The group learns further that Brian had then returned to Dawn, who by this time had given birth to Suzanne, her baby daughter by another man. Ruth, the children's social worker, who was extremely concerned about the situation, kept Dawn under very close review; Dawn, far from resenting this as an intrusion into her private life, greatly valued Ruth as a friend—perhaps the only safe person to whom she could speak about her problem with her family.

Unfortunately, Brian began taking drugs again, and Dawn knew that if she told Ruth, then Suzanne would be taken into care, in addition to the boy who was already fostered.

Dawn declares that she did not want to be dishonest with Ruth, and so, almost exactly one year before (within two days!), she insisted that Brian leave her. Dawn explains how angry yet ambivalent her feelings were for Brian. Her accommodation had been far from satisfactory; it was a house that was let out to various unsettled people, who appeared to occupy single rooms. Supervision was poor. There were fights with the landlord on Friday nights if the rent was not paid; people wandered in and out, drunk, in the early hours. Dawn was caught up in a scuffle one night and taken into custody at the prison. The baby was taken into care for a few days.

The atmosphere in the lodging-house became even worse when Brian attempted to return. Dawn tried to push him away. The baby was crying. Dawn could no longer contain her distress (she had developed a habit of suppressing her frustration because she had felt betrayed in the past when she had disclosed her true feelings; when she could no longer contain them, they exploded in a rush, excessively and uncontrolled). Consequently she got herself drunk and went out, leaving the baby with a friend not noted for her sense of responsibility. She could not explain to Ruth that she was unable to cope with the baby's crying, because the baby was already on an at-risk register and therefore a possible subject for a fit-person order and likely to be taken away. Even so, at a later date Dawn felt betrayed by Ruth when Suzanne was eventually taken into care.

Dawn is now afraid to meet Ruth. Perhaps she is frightened of her own anger towards her, or possibly Dawn has projected her anger into Ruth so that she experiences Ruth as furious with Dawn for not looking after the baby. .

Dawn is then asked to reverse roles with Ruth! From this position, Dawn is able to appreciate the two loyalties of Ruth—one to Dawn, in supporting her with the baby, and the other to her departmental managers, who have a duty to adhere to statutory requirements and to take note of policy guidelines (Fig. 4.1). This discovery is a revelation to Dawn, who until this role reversal has had no clear concept of Ruth's dual responsibilities.

In addition to the role reversal, the director uses Dawn's double, Amanda, to "feed in", indirectly, privileged information. This is not normal practice in classical psychodrama, but in this strategic intervention the overall object is to enable Dawn to meet her social worker in a constructive manner. The double, in response to the director's suggestion, wonders rhetorically, "Has anyone ever looked after me without later letting me down?" Dawn replies that her foster-mother was good to her. Dawn has not seen her for some years and is apprehensive of meeting her again, though she might like to do so, provided she has "support".

The double further protests, "Nobody puts me first; they put the baby first, but never me . . .! How can I say what I really feel when somebody else's needs are always regarded as more important?" This sense of never being given priority is a theme constantly running through Dawn's life.

By the end of the psychodrama, Dawn has made good contact with the group and is able to say that she is feeling more prepared to meet Ruth.

In the sharing phase, Lynn, who has been in the role of Dawn during the role reversal, said that she empathized with Dawn in her loneliness and her need to drink. When asked how she felt as Ruth, the children's social worker, Lynn first said that she had not felt very much; however, while the sharing continued, the realization came upon her that she was in fact very much aware of Dawn's defiance. "That is *me*", Lynn proclaimed. "I can see how I don't

FIGURE 4.1

express my rebelliousness. I bottle it up. I don't realize that it is there and nobody knows about it!" This insight opened up important issues that, in time, Lynn was able to work upon. Also, Lynn, who had a degree related to the social sciences, was later able to say that her own intention had been to become a social worker!

Sequel

The sequel to this psychodrama was that in the afternoon Dawn watched the video of it with her nurse key-worker (Fig. 4.1). A few days later they, together, met Ruth and showed her the video. In this way, Dawn was able to begin resuming her dialogue with Ruth and the children's department.

In time, when the staff were satisfied that she would not get into an uncontrollable rage at meeting her child, she was able to visit Suzanne.

Dawn's difficulty with "facing" those with whom she had fallen out—those she cared greatly for and needed but whom she felt she had let down (or by whom she had felt betrayed)—was a more general feature of her relationship with important people in her life. It was later discovered that she had not been able to "face" her grandmother for three years for fear of telling her that her son had been taken into care.

Summary

This psychodrama, while coming out of the group process during the warm-up, became a vehicle for the director (1) to address a group problem of apparent indifference to staff (later exemplified in Dawn's stubborn defiance), and (2) to enable Dawn to start the process of reconciliation with her social worker, which would result in her being able to visit her baby. The term "strategic" is used here because the director was consciously using the psychodrama as a means for achieving a particular goal in Dawn's overall management. Furthermore, the director was also very controlling with Dawn, following his own agenda rather than that of the protagonist. At what point Dawn understood the director's plan is not clear, nor was the director entirely sure when he had formulated the idea.

Because of Dawn's very stubborn attitude, the director had decided to take a very active lead in the psychodrama. Perhaps this is what the protagonist had needed, since she decided to follow. Although the complementary pattern of "director leading"/"protagonist following" was maintained throughout the action, Dawn gradually became more cooperative.

This style of vigorous management in response to Dawn's defiant passive resistance was part of a pattern that had been in operation throughout her dealings with the children's department and the health services. An early example occurred when she was aged 14; the police had been called in to an indescribably filthy house, to break down the door of Dawn's bedroom when it was thought that she had locked herself inside. They had found her room to be immaculate, amid the squalor of the rest of her mother's house. Dawn had been taken into foster care, which she had valued enormously. Later—about a year after this psychodrama—the director, as Dawn's psychiatrist, decided to visit her grandmother, whom Dawn had not seen for three years, for fear of "breaking her heart" if she found out that Dawn's children were in care. The grandmother, not surprisingly, had been worrying greatly about Dawn and was only too relieved to know that she was in good health. Dawn, once she heard that her grandmother had survived the telling of this news, was only too ready to see her gran, and a visit was soon arranged; in "life", as in the psychodrama, an active initiative was followed eventually by a willing cooperation!

To sum up in systems language: the psychodrama illustrated metaphor and isomorphism. The theme of taking responsibility, first appearing in the warm-up regarding the choice of protagonist, and later referring to a patient's pregnancy, continued into the action phase, where the director finally took over control. This issue eventually became focused upon the children's social worker's responsibility towards Dawn's baby. Dawn's stubbornness could, therefore, be regarded as a disguised sign of her wish for someone to take responsibility for herself, and as a challenge for the group to attempt this. To have acceded to this, however, would have taken the responsibility off Dawn, whereas the purpose of the therapy was to enable her to accept her own accountability. The dilemma was resolved by the group's taking responsibility for itself in relation to Dawn. The psychodrama, then, was a means through which the group members and the director worked together on their joint responsibility for their relationship with Dawn.

Dawn's response was in keeping with this notion. She saw the video in the afternoon and later watched it with Ruth as a way of conveying information that she was otherwise not equipped to impart. The psychodrama, carried out with a protagonist who was initially unable to make a choice, was a metaphor for a mother who takes sufficient responsibility for a child who is not able to make decisions for itself, but doing this only to the extent of enabling the child to see how it can exercise its options.

CHAPTER FIVE

Psychodrama
as a source of information

FORMULATING A SYSTEMIC HYPOTHESIS
IN THE MANAGEMENT OF
A SCHIZOPHRENIC IN-PATIENT

Psychodrama can be useful in securing background information from psychotic patients who, when an ordinary case
history is undertaken, are not able to associate present-day
experiences with past events. When a patient is released from the
question-and-answer format of the formal case history–taking
and given action methods as an accessory language, then, through
the associated changes of role, he can recall and describe events that
are otherwise inaccessible to the conscious mind.

This section demonstrates how clinical signs and family involvement, linked with material from the case history and from the
patient's psychodrama, enable a systemic hypothesis to be made
and to be tested by action at the ward level. The process is illustrated in Figure 5.1 (pp. 84–85).

* * *

81

Edith, a middle-aged lady with chronic schizophrenia, is asked during her psychodrama (Fig. 5.1F) to take on the role of her slightly older brother, who died as a young child; she speaks as if he had been brought back alive to the age that he would be in the present day, had he not died. In her role as the brother, she describes the way that Edith's two older sisters had doted upon him, and how important he was to them in view of the fact that their mother, overwhelmed by their alcoholic, tyrannical father, was not emotionally available to them. The sisters were devastated when the brother died, and they switched their attention to Edith to fill the gap. One of the sisters later had an illegitimate child, presumably in an attempt to have someone of her own to love rather than to have to share Edith with her sister. This was before the Second World War. Two close relatives had committed suicide, one out of grief following the death of her own child. The family shame at what, at the time, they felt to be unspeakable events—illegitimacy and suicide—isolates them from other people. They had also found these matters impossible to speak about as children, even within the family.

Six years after this psychodrama, Edith was readmitted with negative catatonic signs; she was mute and refused to eat or to get out of bed (Fig. 5.1A).

Searching for a systemic hypothesis to account for Edith's relapse and for the form it has taken, the psychiatrist tried to link present-day family relationships with what had been learnt in the psychodrama. At family sessions, the sisters seemed reluctant to talk in depth about their family background.

The sisters were noted to be frequent visitors to Edith on the ward, where they often came at the same time. It was discovered that when Edith was at home, the sisters maintained regular and frequent contact with Edith, but not with each other.

It also emerged that there was a potential for conflict between these close sisters over the need of one to rely upon the other for financial advice. From time to time the sisters had their own problems, which they were unable to share with each other. Edith, however, was a focal point: if the sisters required contact with one another, Edith's hospital admission gave them a "reason" to meet up. Furthermore, by concerning themselves with Edith, they displaced their own worries onto her.

The hypothesis (Fig. 5.1*H*) was made that when the sisters had their own troubles (such as illness or conflict with their children), they communicated with Edith and about Edith. Edith may well have found it stressful to be on the receiving end. Confusion might have contributed to her relapse—she was not clear whether the sisters were solicitous for her or were making use of her illness as a means to manage their own distress. Both might have been true. Edith's mutism, food refusal, and hospitalization might have indicated that Edith was both wishing to be admitted to hospital and yet at the same time protesting at her medical care. She wanted relief from the anxieties of her sisters, and yet she wished to be available for her sisters' needs. Edith's compromise, in the face of the paradox of both "wanting" to be visited and yet also not "wanting" to be visited, was to be admitted to hospital, but not to be able to talk—the sisters could visit and meet each other, but they could not talk to Edith since Edith did not converse.

The systemic meaning of Edith's mutism and the paradoxical nature of her catatonic signs could therefore be explained by her profound ambivalence towards her sisters and to being looked after in hospital.

In family sessions, the sisters and their husbands attended (but never both husbands at the same time; legitimate reasons were given, but it was postulated that there might have been some conflict between them). Some of their own separate anxieties were addressed, but there was great resistance to this; they wanted to focus upon Edith's illness (Fig. 5.1*G*). When it was perceived that the more they did this, the more intense Edith's ambivalence over being "ill" would become, a structural/strategic intervention was made (Fig. 5.1*I*): the sisters' visiting Edith on the ward was restricted, and they were to visit Edith only when she was at her own home (to which the community psychiatric nurse was taking her for increasing periods of time during the day).

This plan was successful. Edith had calibrated the relationship between her sisters since her childhood insofar as they had, together, given the time and love to Edith that they had been unable to get from their mother. Edith had also filled the gap when her brother had died. Between her psychodrama and her relapse six years later, their mother had died, and Edith had once again filled a

EDITH Aged 60

SCHIZOPHRENIA   (Negative Catatonic)

A.   PRESENTATION

Psychiatric Hospital

Mute
Refusal to eat
Refusal to get out of bed.

Visited by two
elder sisters.

B.   HISTORY OF PSYCHIATRIC ILLNESS.

AGE	PSYCHIATRIC ILLNESS
35	Depression after broken marriage
40	**Neurotic Anorexia** 2 years lying on bed at home – losing weight
43	**Schizophrenia Diagnosed** 10 years on oral neuroleptic drugs Working as P.A. to a prominent civil servant
53	RELAPSE. Stops work. looks after mother. (Father is dead.) Does a psychodrama.
54	Mother dies. Patient lives independently at home.
58/59	Repeated admissions

C.   CONNECTION BETWEEN A & B?   Edith's relationship with her sisters.

D.   WHAT IS MISSING?   An understanding of Edith's sisters.

E.   WHAT HELPS GIVE A MEANING TO EDITH'S PRESENTING MENTAL STATE?

F   EDITH'S   PSYCHODRAMA (INFORMATION IN RETROSPECT).
(aged 53)

Takes the role of her brother, who died in childhood, before Edith was born.

Using **SURPLUS REALITY** she speaks as though his spirit is still alive and she recalls memories and provides material that neither her sisters, nor Edith in her normal role, would discuss.

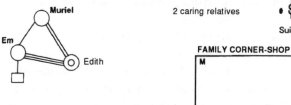

2 caring relatives

Suicide   Suicide

FAMILY CORNER-SHOP

FIGURE 5.1

84

G   FAMILY SESSIONS

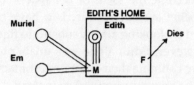

Sisters' grief over death
of mother turns to caring
for Edith.

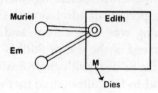

But: who is lookng after whom?

H

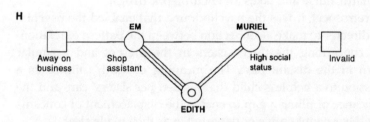

HYPOTHESIS:

1. Edith calibrates the relationship between Em and Muriel.

2. But if Edith alone is unable to manage this the 'structure' of the Psychiatric Hospital helps her with this role.

I   INTERVENTION:

1. Visiting times of sisters to the ward is restricted.

then

2. Sisters are only to visit Edith when she is at her home.

    (Edith is taken to her home, by Community Psychiatric Nurse, for increasing periods of time).

gap, to become the focus of her sisters' concern. The unconscious family belief system appeared to have been that grief was to be mitigated by looking after a substitute figure.

If, however, Edith alone was unable to contain her sisters' distress or to calibrate their emotional contact, then the structure of the hospital as an institution did so instead. Unfortunately, such a pattern could become self-perpetuating (there had been a succession of ever-increasing periods of admission to the ward, until the overall systemic meaning was deciphered), and it was dysfunctional. By becoming deprived of the use of Edith's illnesses and hospitalization as a vehicle to deal with their anxiety and grief, the sisters presumably had to find alternative methods; since the final intervention, Edith has been living in her own home independently and without significant symptoms. She has visits from the community psychiatric nurse and takes oral neuroleptic drugs.

In retrospect, it was the psychodrama that enabled the psychiatrist/director to make a connection between the pattern of relationships concerning the three sisters in the present and a similar pattern in the distant past. The meaning of Edith's illness as a regression to a helpless child that needed her sisters' care and the significance of filling a gap to enable the displacement of concerns about other people, alive or departed, was then made clear.

The psychodrama six years previously may well have helped Edith directly at the time, but in this case its most obvious significance was in helping the psychiatrist to construct a systemic hypothesis to account for Edith's relapses. From a theoretical viewpoint, regarding Edith's own psychopathology, it was amazing how spontaneous Edith had been in the role of her brother, compared with the stilted and predictable manner that she had acquired over the years (she had been diagnosed as having schizophrenia ten years before her psychodrama and had been on continuous medication during that time). The idea that Edith herself had remained identified all her life with her dead brother, in her family's unconscious mind as well as in her own, would account both for her life-long lack of sense of self, culminating in schizophrenia, and also, ironically, for the spontaneity that she exhibited in the role of her brother!

THE DIAGNOSIS OF
POST–TRAUMATIC STRESS DISORDER

Danielle, a lady in her late forties, has been attending the mental health services intermittently for twenty-two years. She had originally presented as a heavily dependent, highly anxious, phobic, and histrionic personality. Early on, she had managed to persuade her father-in-law to escort her to group therapy sessions and even to wait to take her home. She had had a very ambivalent relationship with a possessive father and an overprotective mother, and she had left her parents in Belgium to come and live in Guernsey, although she could not cope on her own. It was thought that she exhibited separation anxiety, compounded with a need to differentiate herself from her mother and father to prevent herself from becoming caught up in her parents' marital conflict. One result of her needing to retain her individual identity, while having at the same time profound dependent needs, was that as soon as any therapist appeared to be getting too close, she would disappear for a time, only to be referred to some new doctor or team worker.

In the warm-up of a psychodrama session (Fig. 5.2) she again gave conflicting messages. One of these was that she had "butterflies". The other was that she was "not ready" to work on her problem. Group members confronted her: how would she know when she was ready? Danielle exhibited an enviable degree of stubbornness in refusing to be persuaded, until she made "a deal": she would be the protagonist if she could first spend five minutes in the toilet.

The context of the warm-up was probably very relevant: Danielle was expressing the group's own preoccupation with the passing of the old year and its ambivalent feelings about the new (this was the first psychodrama of the New Year). There was a determination to make more of it than the previous year, but this was mixed with wariness about once more facing sadness, pain, work, and conflict. It was a fight/flight attitude, expressed by members more in relation towards the future than to one another.

At the beginning of her psychodrama, Danielle's fear of palpitations appears in the context of an isolated, futile existence at her home, where she hoovers and dusts repetitively and excessively,

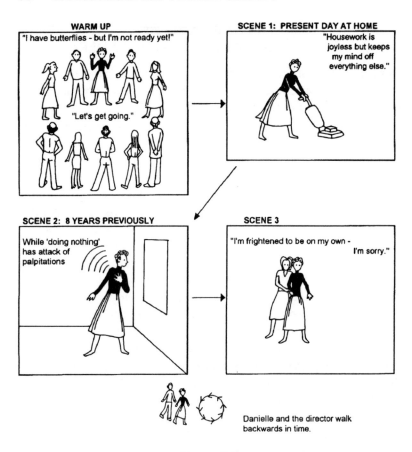

FIGURE 5.2

with no joy in her work. In fact, the tedium and the distaste of "doing" her work serve to deflect her mind from all other thoughts or feelings. The scene changes to when the panics began in the same room of her house eight years previously; her palpitations occur "out of the blue" as she is looking out of the window at nothing in particular. (Perhaps it is, indeed, relevant that she is actually *not* "doing" anything at the time.) She has a great fear of being on her own, and she seeks the company of a younger neighbour—without, however, "admitting" that she has palpitations until later, when she meets an older woman who is more likely to be able to cope. There Danielle bursts into tears and apologizes—as though making a "confession" to a capable woman that she is sad and frightened.

FIGURE 5.2 *(continued)*

Danielle is then taken to a scene further back in time through the technical and metaphorical procedure of walking hand-in-hand with the director in an anti-clockwise circle. Danielle comes to a stop at the age of 13. She is fleeing from Africa with her parents at the time of a Colonial Civil War. People are committing suicide and are jumping out of ships as they leave their homeland. Danielle "sees" this again as she describes the scene and then shakes with fear and howls with grief. She needs physical holding by the director. He asks her whether she has ever spoken of this before, and she shakes her head.

After a time, she goes back to a scene where she is aged 9 in her maternal grandmother's large flat in the capital city. Her grandmother and her mother are in conflict. Danielle admires and loves both of them. She is the fifth child of seven and the first daughter, her father's favourite. He is a proud upper-class chauvinist who nevertheless compels his family to live in his mother-in-law's apartment because of his insolvency; he has been a play-boy who had only begun to make a career when Danielle was born. (Is Danielle— a daughter—what the whole family had needed in order to function? Had mother continued having babies in the hope of having a female child, to get father working?) In the role of various members of her family, Danielle is asked to speak in Flemmish, her own tongue, which intensifies a sense of immediacy.

Danielle has a great sense of responsibility, which is particularly called forth when the argument between mother and grandmother reaches a crescendo. Mother states, "I will do as I please", and then falls to the ground, lying motionless in a faint. Danielle, tearful, believes her to be dead. She grasps a statue of the Virgin, places it upon her mother's chest, and prays.

Danielle then refers to the two following years; she states: "I did things no one would believe of a child." There were the horrors of civil war and of terrorism—of secrets that, if not kept, would lead to the murder of the betrayer. Homes were lost, lives ruined, and families broken up.

The director realizes that ever since that time Danielle has been suffering from post–traumatic stress disorder. The horror of thinking that she saw her mother die and the terrors of a civil war were superimposed upon a family conflict, which Danielle experienced as revolving around herself. It is likely that one situation intensified the other. The dilemma for the family as a whole was whether or not to leave their African homeland and, later, when to depart. The parents' other quandary was whether or not to stick together. Danielle was the common link; mother, grandmother, and father all thought very highly of Danielle, and as the first daughter she had a special position as one both cherished and looked upon to keep everyone else happy.

For their psychological survival, the Belgian ex-patriates had to hold together, keeping up their morale by adopting a group "defiance", as Danielle had put it. This was true both for the community at large and for the family. An equivalent of the "stiff upper-lip" was the inner individual defiance that matched that of the family and the group—to allow oneself to become frightened or distressed risked revealing it to others, which would be an act of disloyalty and would erode the solidarity of the people. It was no wonder that Danielle was "stubborn" in the warm-up. She was not in the habit of letting her fear and sadness show. During the original attack of palpitations eight years previously, she had not even spoken of her racing heart to her young neighbour, whom she felt she might have upset. She had even apologized to the director, as though her tears were a "confession" of feelings she felt she should not possess; she was apparently concerned lest this display of crying would be putting a responsibility unfairly on to someone else.

Typical of the situation that gives rise to post–traumatic stress disorder is fear coupled with an inability at the time to do anything practical about the stress—either to fight it or to alleviate it, especially for other people. Another characteristic is the inability to share at the time the feelings of panic, pain, and despair with others. This was Danielle's situation. The result was a suppression of these feelings or a denial of their existence. Often, as in Danielle's case, feelings are repressed from conscious memory, at the cost of haunting the subject in the form of drug-resistant depression, generalized anxiety, nightmares, phobias, or bodily symptoms; very often the link between the symptoms and the original stress is outside of awareness.

To help Danielle to begin to work through the stress, the director took up the subject of Danielle's father, who, he had learned early in the psychodrama, had died four years previously. Danielle had referred to an object in her front room, which was a gift from her father. The director, having enabled Danielle to relive consciously some of the traumatic episodes of her childhood and to be aware of how to make sense of her symptoms, needed to help Danielle *deal* with her distress. One method already employed was that of catharsis: to reexperience the trauma, while at the same time allowing her true feelings to be expressed, before doing something positive about the situation. Another method would be to enable her to share her feelings with her family members—something that a child would have needed to do to feel protected and comforted.

Danielle is asked whether there was any conversation with her father she would have liked to have had before he had died. She readily agrees to invent a scene with her father that could have taken place if he were still alive. She chooses a private spot outdoors in Belgium. She had not told her father directly that she loved him, and she wishes to take this opportunity. In reverse-role, as father, she says that he is proud of his daughter; he was not an easy man to live with, and he did not always do what he should have done as a husband or a father, but he has always loved and cherished his daughter. Back in her normal role, Danielle listens to the auxiliary as her father repeats this. She is overcome with tears of joy to hear it, and she experiences a profound sadness that this is also their farewell. They give each other a final hug, and the group gathers around to share.

A member of the group speaks of the difficulties she had in dealing with her love for a father who had been cruel to her. Another talks of a recent conversation with her father that she had made a point of having after her own psychodrama. A third woman talks of her difficulty in ever speaking personally or privately to her father, knowing that he will always inform her mother of what she says to him.

* * *

In psychiatric terms, this psychodrama was about the diagnosis and management of post–traumatic stress disorder. From a psychodynamic perspective, it was about denial, displacement, and repetition compulsion: the patient tried endlessly to repeat the trauma in the hope of mastering it, only to continue to fail. In systems language, it was also about isomorphism and metaphor. The pattern of her present life-style represents her time in Africa, when she could not go out of the house. Her stubbornness, as shown in the warm-up, would indicate a continuing need to feel in control in what is still seen as a very threatening world. Her panic and palpitations symbolize the perceived death of her mother and are also a somatic equivalent of the psychological stress that she could not show to people in the present day—a repitition of the past, when everyone had to be brave together. Her relationship with the hospital and staff over the years could also be viewed as representing, or being symbolic of, her relationship with her family in her late childhood: an over-dependence arising from the threat of outside danger, with a need to escape in reaction to this (shown by switching therapists or doctors), to avoid a conflict of loyalties between herself and parental figures.

CHAPTER SIX

Summary:
the effect of
one therapy role upon another
in a public mental health service

This book presents clinical material from the viewpoint of a psychiatrist, a psychodrama practitioner, or a family therapist, depending upon the stance required at any particular time. Situations might arise with one individual patient, a therapy group, or a family. Reference was made in chapter one to the ways in which individual team members, also, can adjust their roles according to the task with which the clinical team is presented. One manifestation of isomorphism (see de Shazer, 1982, for an account of this phenomenon) is the propensity of a therapeutic team, or of a network of agencies, to replicate the conflicting attitudes that operate in the presenting family.

Awareness of this phenomenon is helpful in the diagnosis or understanding of how the family operates, not only in relation to the team members or agencies, but within the family system itself, and particularly how the family might function if the agencies did not exist. A similar operation was applied in Balint's (1964) groups of family doctors, where the feelings engendered within the group during the discussion of a case were utilized to assist the case-presenter in understanding his own response to the patient and in adopting the appropriate therapeutic stance.

In analytic psychotherapy, the therapist alone may need to recognize and contain the patient's projections by becoming aware of the feelings engendered in himself in response to communication with the patient. In this way the therapist can sense the feelings that the patient finds too painful to experience, using this knowledge as diagnostic information and the process as a container for the patient's anxieties.

It is also possible (as I shall explain in a later book) for a whole system of mental health care to organize itself so that it can be sensitive to the different ways in which cases are presented—whether as individuals, as family referrals, or as complex problems including different agencies. If the system is flexible enough, as is possible in a small community, to take account of previous experiences with the patient or family, then such information about how the health-care system was affected by the presentation or referral can be utilized by the team as a whole in deciding upon the appropriate response.

To be thus effective, the team must have the ability to communicate within itself, and the member most concerned with the patient at any particular time must be able to adopt the appropriate stance, according to the team's formulation. This may entail a community psychiatric nurse (CPN) becoming a social inquirer and information-seeker at one point, and a distance-regulator (as in adjusting the amount of time spent between a patient and his family) at another. This CPN would be able to utilize these two roles as much by virtue of his personal rapport with the family as through administrative convenience.

Edith's case, in chapter five, illustrates the kind of psychiatric work that entails utilizing previous experiences of a patient, including material from a psychodrama, to enable the team, patient, and family to resolve an emotional dilemma and to allow the clinical features of the problem to be dispelled.

For some complex cases, especially those involving a number of interacting elements, as with Edith, more than one intervention is required. With others, even long-standing ones, an intervention using only one therapeutic modality can appear to suffice. In contrast to Edith's case, which required the physical structure of the hospital and the active intervention of the CPN, Danielle's case, also from chapter five, is an example of how psychodrama alone appears to effect a major change in some patients when family members are not available and when a patient of her own free will attends the day unit specifically for group therapy and psychodrama.

Psychodrama can sometimes be regarded as an instrument for "playing with time". Boundaries of time and place are defined and re-defined, allowing events to be arranged and rearranged according to the various meanings given to them by protagonist, director, and group members. Different patterns of time connect these three parties as the drama is socially created and reconstituted in a recursive fashion.

By separating out the components of Danielle's present-day concerns (and their physiological accompaniments) according to their different origins in time—by stretching the 90 minutes of psychodramatic action to cover a period of 30 years—the "meaning" of her experience is given a historical context: its implication for Danielle in the past defines its later significance. It is only when Danielle "sees" anew her "forgotten" past and, moreover, when for the first time she "speaks" of it, that she is able to see its connection with her current life concerns.

Furthermore, she can only now "speak", because she has found, in the moment of her psychodrama, a present-day context in which it is safe, relevant, and appropriate to talk of the horrific events and agonizing dilemmas of her past. Loyalties to her relatives and the dangers of civil war had contrived to silence her, without her even realizing this, since, to cope alone with her experiences, she had been forced to keep back memories, even from her own conscious mind. The changing of the time-frame in the psychodrama had enabled Danielle to venture back to the period before the imposition of her allegiances of loyalty, and to free her to express to the group members—especially those in auxiliary roles—what she as a child had been unable to state: her anger at being expected by her parents and grandparents to be responsible for mediating the family's internal conflicts in her role as the first daughter and the specially valued child of both parties. She was the helpless observer of both the civil war and the family's hostilities—isomorphic patterns, where the effect of one seemed to reinforce the other.

She was able in a second psychodrama some weeks later to express this anger more forcefully and, once more, to "resurrect" her father and talk with him about the sorrow and grief that his defensive attitude had rendered impossible for her to share with him in life. Thereafter, she had been able to begin to lay to rest, "buried" with him, her hitherto "unfinished business".

Danielle might have recalled the same forgotten scenes under hypnosis, and she could have "relived" the emotional turmoil by way of an abreaction with intravenous amylobarbitone, but her catharsis would have been entirely personal. In a psychoanalytic framework it would have been interpersonal, the therapist perhaps representing a parent, through the transference. However, psychodrama was able to provide Danielle with the opportunity to view herself in the situation she had been in from the position of other family members as well as from her own perspective; her predicament was both subjectively and objectively apprehended. The group members—and Danielle herself, in role-reversal—gave permission for Danielle to tell her story, to relive the experience, and to set it into words.

Experience committed to words that others can hear is of a different order from that which is not articulated. Through the magic of language, through words uttered in the company of people who are known to perceive and understand their meaning, thoughts can be "made flesh".

When the director, speaking for the whole group with the assent and acknowledgement of all those present, sets a scene, it has, through its shared meaning, a socially created reality: it is experienced as an "actual" scene, for it is at one and the same time the "same" scene for the protagonist, the director, and the group. The auxiliary mother, fallen to the floor and feared to be dead, *is* symbolically Danielle's mother, and Danielle's response is socially authentic. It is not merely "acting"—at that particular time she is truly Danielle.

The most fundamental property of action as drama, however, is the degree of involvement of the group members. They do not just observe, as the director might observe the whole system, including, hopefully, himself as a part of it (Von Foerster, 1979) They, too, are psychically "in" the drama. Danielle as a child, for example, resonates, by identification, with the "child" in all the group members. Her pain is their pain. Her catharsis is also theirs. Moreover, it is in particular the unwanted or unacknowledged aspects of themselves that come to light in the most intense dramas. The needy child, the abusive persecutor, the socially unacceptable outcast in all of us are represented in the protagonist's story, sometimes unconsciously but often brought into awareness. The protagonist does the "work" not only of himself, but also of the group members.

Besides enabling an individual to "work" on behalf of others, a psychodrama can perform the function of "recycling" of a portion of what a society has branded as its "refuse". Thus, the concept of the mental health institution as a container for reclaiming the cast-off aspects of a society can be examined in microcosm in Lucy's psychodrama in chapter three. The subject of social status is studied and resolved through a drama that Lucy carries out on behalf of the group, and in this process she detoxifies the projections and introjections that lead to scapegoating.

We have seen how, in the sociometric warm-up to Lucy's psychodrama, the social "outcast" becomes the "chosen one"—a pattern that is replicated in the action phase. The conversion of Lucy into becoming the chosen protagonist takes place only because a transmogrification occurs at the same time in the group-as-a-whole: each member is to some extent transformed within himself; the unacceptable parts are, consciously or otherwise, felt, and to a greater or lesser extent, personally "owned".

This transmutation, or reversal, through drama, has another bearing on the role of public mental health institutions. Psychiatric hospitals are frequently imbued with a degree of social stigma, and much has been written about the social uses made of psychiatric staff if political authority is brought to bear upon the management of asylums and their residents. Foucault (1971) described various attitudes to mental asylums according to their historical periods, though the accuracy of his historical research is disputed by Merquior (1985). Different attitudes to "madness" also appear to prevail within small communities than in larger ones.

The family, in particular, may be the first group to select one of its members to be the "identified patient". However, the family may not by any means disown the patient. Indeed, psychiatric patients are typically characterized as being either the objects of too much conscious family concern or the recipients of too little, when they are isolated in a hospital and forgotten about. Both patterns are most clearly evident at visiting times, when some patients have a superfluity of visitors and others, like Dawn in chapter four, hardly any. Some patients are sociometric "stars" and some are isolates. Some are regarded with great concern as distressed, ill, and "suffering", while others are relegated to the position of outcasts who are not supposed to experience their own humanity with the true depth of feeling of "normal" people.

This selection is not, however, solely determined by the other family members. The patient also plays a part in this discrimination, mental health law certification notwithstanding. From a systems perspective, the patient and family can be regarded as one holon or "system within a system" (see Minuchin & Fishman, 1981, for a description of this term, taken from Arthur Koestler), whether or not the patient is in the hospital. Even though the patient may not consciously "choose" to be in hospital, he contains within himself, isomorphically, like a hologram, all of the parts of the wider family system and succumbs, in psychodynamic terms, to carrying on behalf of the family its unwanted parts. In systems terms, the family seeks to resolve an emotional dilemma by confining one of its members within a boundary away from the family home; it resorts to "action". Usually when undertaken in a family context, an admission is brought about when there has been an escalation (an uninterrupted period of positive feedback) in the family's communication system. The system has gone into "runaway" and a vicious circle has been set in motion. Hospital admission provides the overdue punctuation.

Admission to a psychiatric hospital, furthermore, has a number of other functions in relation to family crises. Sometimes a patient may be regarded as one of a dyad, such as a spouse pair, that requires the hospital to be a reference point to help regulate its interactions. The hospital becomes the third point of a triangle, which is needed, according to Bowen (1978) to restore stability to any dyad. Usually, however, the patient himself is the one that is initially triangulated. For Edith, in chapter five, there appeared no other possible course of action but to be "insane"—a condition that would lead to action, since insanity was incompatible with the rules, expectations, or needs of other family members. Edith may not have realized that she was unable to tolerate spending more time with one sister than another, if one of them was in need of more support than Edith could provide. Had she had this insight, Edith could not have "rejected" her sister by telling her this. Neither could she have betrayed either sister by saying that one was neglecting the other. She could only resolve this by becoming admitted to hospital, when the third sister would have been involved of her own accord.

The function of the psychiatric hospital for those more obviously making a conscious choice to be there appears different from those who are "confined" in it when they are psychotic. Dawn, in chapter four, was eventually admitted because she had become an isolate and could not cope with loneliness. It was not culturally possible in that particular community to "complain" of loneliness; there were no organizations that provided supervised hostels for young "normal" adults. To "qualify" for hostel accommodation, it was necessary to be ill or alcoholic! Dawn developed prolonged psychogenic fainting spells that "forced" the doctors to take action; they could not leave her lying on the floor of her flat!

The mental health institution can, therefore, be seen as having a fostering parental function: it accepts people for periods of time to contain anxieties, and, by providing physical boundaries, it operates a "holding" function until the family or an alternative body can re-assimilate them. Dawn was encouraged to advertise in the local press for a family that would take her in, like a fostered adult. She was immediately successful. Clearly, she had needed for herself what her own children were given as they had become "toddlers" and taken into care.

We have seen that psychodrama can be viewed as an enactment that can lead to a transformation in the experience of self and of the standing of self in the eyes of the group. Many psychiatric hospital admissions are also experienced as dramatic enactments. There is action (the admission) and there is a heightened exaggeration of roles: a first admission, at least, is hardly a routine matter in the lives of most patients and their families! On the other hand, it is not the end of the story. It is an intermission and there are other acts to be played out, including the transformation and the reconciliation. Almost all patients eventually leave hospital, but some gain more from the experience than do others. Some, with their families, can positively benefit from the physical boundary of the hospital if its significance is understood by all those who have drawn it or who have been otherwise involved in its delineation. If the ward case-review with the family can be seen in some ways as equivalent to the psychodrama stage, then the interaction between family and patient can be regulated by the staff in a manner that is analogous to the way in which a psychodrama director manages the stage. The role of the hospital is purposely modified to co-create a dialogue with the patient and the family.

A disguised and rarely acknowledged purpose for admission to a psychiatric ward may be to provide a physical boundary between a patient and his family or friends. In a small, highly defined community in an age of refined communications technology, ease of communication renders insulation from surplus or unwanted contact with relatives difficult. In such highly interactive communities, more rigid social boundaries have to be established to make up for the effect of more permeable physical borders. Without these social constraints, there would be chaos; it is difficult for a person to avoid communicating if others insist upon it. Complex inter-generational connections can render people vulnerable to so many multiple evaluations that they become confused in their sense of self.

When communication is excessively distorted, the public psychiatric service is sometimes required to take action rather than to rely entirely upon dialogue. In a small community, however, action—by way of hospital admission—may now be of a different order. Whereas once it was viewed as indiscriminately restrictive and constraining, today it is coming to be seen as more responsive to quite different and various individual needs through an understanding of patients, families, and problems in terms of systems theory. Hospital admission provides a structure for those lacking this as much as it forcibly extracts someone from an already existing rigid entanglement. Furthermore, by providing a setting for families to meet for sessions and a stage for psychodrama, it creates a means for putting systemic thinking into action.

If the institution of the family is changing and the father's role is being taken up more by the State as fathers are unemployed or need their wives to work to maintain the family, and if women are coming to see social security as more "secure" than husbands, the State is likely to be faced with an increasing paternal responsibility. However, in the home itself single mothers often have to assume a greater share of fatherly functions and can perhaps therefore give less as mothers. The mental health services were typically seen as masculine hierarchical structures—maintained, like an army, by rules, regulations, and sanctions. Today, however, there is fortunately also a feminine responsivity in State-run "care"; the "maturational process and the facilitating environment" (Winnicott, 1965) may have come into their own, metaphorically, in the public domain of adult mental health!

We have seen a number of examples of how a clinical team can adapt to the particular requirements that individual patients and their families may have of a public mental health service. We have also observed how, over a period of time, different therapeutic modalities can be accommodated to the individual needs of the patient, family, or group at any particular moment.

Finally, having discussed the importance of a therapeutic modality in accommodating to the particular needs of a patient or family in finding options for the most appropriate approaches, it remains once more to consider the importance of flexibility in the role of the therapist or psychiatrist. If he is practising individual psychoanalytic therapy and the patient is able to benefit from it, then in a public service the resources of time available might be a limiting factor. If, however, the patient presents because of pressure from other family members, then individual therapy could be difficult insofar as a therapist might be expected to help resolve problems that do not reside entirely within the patient. Furthermore, if the patient is referred to a psychiatric hospital with symptoms carried on behalf of other family members (if, for example, he is bearing the burden of a family's unresolved grief), then the psychiatrist/therapist must find ways to address the issues directly with the relevant family members. Some patients present systemic problems in psychodrama or other kinds of groups. Others are observed to "coast" as regular attenders, but without significant progress unless a systems approach is adopted. Patients who are severely ill and who require active ward management for a psychotic reaction or for some other crisis also need to have their situation viewed from a systemic perspective.

The psychiatrist/therapist must apply a therapeutic stance not only in accordance with the perceived needs of the patient, but also taking into account the wider system of public mental health care, of which the clinician is a part. To maintain the appropriate role of systems operator, this position is crucial. There are three requirements: (1) The clinician must attend to his own spontaneity, much as a psychodrama director responds to new situations in appropriate ways or to old problems by novel means (Moreno, 1953). (2) If the clinician works within the structure of an institution, he must use it creatively. In the context of physical structure, account must be taken of the various needs required of it: those of the patient, the family, the referring agents, and moreover, the hospital staff, whose own anxieties must be acknowledged. (3) A systems operator must be able to adapt his role to integrate the client systems and the service systems (including the hospital), with the systems of therapy, so that these latter are applied in interventions appropriate to the clinical needs and to the resources available to attend to them. Fruggeri (1991) explains how the importance of interpretations, interventions, or techniques lies in the context of what they contribute to the total therapeutic impact upon the patient.

Conducting psychodrama is analogous to operating as a systems therapist in a more general frame of reference. Without using the same language, psychodrama has been shown to utilize systems principles. What it also provides in its own right is the concept of attending, through action methods, to the roles through which people communicate, and, in turn, affect the way that others express themselves. In other words, if a particular meaning is ascribed to action while it is being taken, some roles can change and in turn influence other roles. The director attends first to his own actions and their meanings, and, provided that he maintains his own spontaneity, he can elicit spontaneity from others. As Hollander (1992) points out, Bowen's theory centres around differentiation, while for Moreno spontaneity is at the heart of the individual's uniqueness. In thinking systemically while attending to his own stance, the director of psychodrama defines his role in relation to the other group members, and through this process he also helps them to define their own roles. As Williams (1989) points out, Moreno understood the systemic nature of roles, including their context and consequences.

* * *

Psychodrama as presented in this book is a specific method of therapy that can be combined and coordinated with many other methods; some of its principles, however, also serve as a model for a systems therapist in the general field of mental health care, as I shall show in another book. It exemplifies the way in which a therapist or psychiatrist can attend to his therapeutic role-repertoire and examine his own system of ideas for conducting therapy while he is in the process of taking "action"—whether this be physical, such as to provide a holding environment, or verbal, as by way of conversation or interpretation. Therapeutic interventions usually involve both and thus often reflect the effect of one therapy role upon another in a public mental health service.

REFERENCES AND BIBLIOGRAPHY

Agazarian, Y. (1993). "A Theory of Living Human Systems and the Practice of Systems-Centred Psychotherapy." Special presentation at the Thirty-Seventh Annual Meeting of the American Group Psychotherapy Association.

Anderson, H. (in press). Collaborative Language Systems: Toward a Postmodern Therapy. In: R. Mikesell, D. D. Lusterman, and S. McDaniel (Eds.), *Family Psychology and Systems Theory*. Washington, DC: American Psychological Association Press.

Anderson, H., Goolishian, A., & Windermand, L. (1987). Problem-Determined Systems: Towards Transformation in Family Therapy. *Journal of Strategic and Systemic Therapies, 5*: 1–14.

Andolfi, N., Angelo, C., Menghi, P., & Nicolò-Congliano, A. M. (1983). *Behind the Family Mask*. New York: Brunner/Mazel.

Balint, M. (1964). *The Doctor, His Patient and the Illness*. London: Pitman Medical.

Bandler, R., & Grinder, J. (1975). *Patterns of the Hypnotic Techniques of Milton H. Erickson, Vol. 1*. Cupertino, CA: Meta Publications.

Bateson, G. (1979). *Mind and Nature: A Necessary Unity*. London: Fontana.

Beck, A. T., Rush, A. J., Shaf, B. F., & Emery, G. (1979). *Cognitive Therapy of Depression*. New York: Brunner/Mazel.

Bentovim, A. (1992). *Trauma-Organized Systems: Physical and Sexual Abuse in Families*. London: Karnac Books [revised edition, 1995].

Bion, W. (1962). *Learning from Experience*. London: Heinemann.

Blatner, A., & Blatner A. (1988). *Foundations of Psychodrama, History Theory and Practice*. New York: Springer Publishing.

Bollas, C. (1987). *The Shadow of the Object; Psychoanalysis of the Unknown Thought*. London: Free Association Books.

Boscolo, L., Cecchin, G., Campbell, D., & Draper, R. (1985). Twenty More Questions: Selections from a Discussion between the Milan Associates and the Editors. In: D. Campbell & R. Draper (Eds.), *Applications of Systemic Family Therapy, The Milan Approach* (chapter 27). New York: Grune & Stratton.

Boszormenyi-Nagy, I. (1981). Contextual Therapy: Therapeutic Leverages in Mobilizing Trust. In: R. J. Green. & J. L. Fram (Eds.), *Family Therapy, Major Contributions*. New York: International Universities Press.

Bowen, M. (1978). *Family Therapy in Clinical Practice*. New York: Jason Aronson.

Brittan, A. (1973). *Meanings and Situations*. International Library of Sociology, John Rex (Ed.). London/Boston: Routledge & Kegan Paul.

Campbell, D., Draper, R., & Huffington, C. (1989). *Second Thoughts on the Theory and Practice of the Milan Approach to Family Therapy*. London: D.C. Associates.

Chasin, R., Roth, S., & Bograd, N. (1989). Action Methods in Systemic Therapy: Dramatising Ideal Futures and Reformed Pasts with Couples. *Family Process, 28*: 121–136.

Compernolle, T. (1981). J. L. Moreno: An Unrecognized Pioner of Family Therapy. *Family Process, 20*: 331–335.

de Shazer, S. (1982). *Patterns of Brief Family Therapy*. New York: Guilford Press.

de Shazer, S. (1991). *Putting Difference to Work*. New York: W. W. Norton.

Dicks, H. V. (1967). *Marital Tensions*. London: Routledge & Kegan Paul.

Epston, D., & White, M. (1990). *Archaeology of Therapy*. South Australia: Dulwich Centre Publications.

Fogarty, T. F. (1978). The Distancer and Pursuer. In: *The Best of the Family 1973–1978, Vol. 7*. (No. 1). New Rochelle, NY: The Centre for Family Learning.

Foucault, M. (1971). *Madness and Civilization: A History of Insanity in the Age of Reason.* London: Tavistock.

Fox, J. (Ed.) (1987). *The Essential Moreno: Writings on Psychodrama, Group Method, and Spontaneity by J. L. Moreno, M.D.* New York: Springer Publishing.

Framo, J. L. (1982). *Explorations in Marital and Family Therapy: Selected Papers of James L. Framo.* New York: Springer.

Fruggeri, L. (1991). The Constructivist Systemic Approach and Context Analysis. In: L. Fruggeri et al., *New Systemic Ideas from the Italian Mental Health Movement.* London: Karnac Books.

Fruggeri, L., & Matteini, M. (1991). From Dualism to Complexity: Methodological Issues in Psychotherapy in Public Services. In: L. Fruggeri et al., *New Systemic Ideas from the Italian Mental Health Movement.* London: Karnac Books.

Ganzarain, R. C., & Buchele, B. J. (1989). *Fugitives of Incest: A Perspective from Psychoanalysis and Groups.* Madison, CT: International Universities Press.

Goldman, E., & Morrison, D. (1984). *Pyschodrama: Experience and Processs.* Dubuque, IA: Kendall/Hunt.

Guerin, P. J., Jr. (1976). Family Therapy: The First Twenty Five Years. In: P. J. Guerin, Jr. (Ed.), *Family Therapy: Theory and Practice.* New York: Gardner Press.

Havens, L. (1986). *Making Contact: Uses of Language in Psychotherapy.* Cambridge, MA: Harvard University Press.

Hinshelwood, R. D., & Manning, N. (1979). *Therapeutic Communities, Reflections and Progress.* London: Routledge & Kegan Paul.

Hinshelwood, R. D. (1987). *What Happens in Groups? Psychoanalysis, the Individual and the Community.* London: Free Association Books.

Holland, R. (1977). *Self and Social Context.* London: Macmillan.

Hollander, C. E. (1992). *Psychodrama, Role-Playing, and Sociometry: Living and Learning Processes. Comparative Family Systems of Moreno and Bowen.* Lakewood, CO: Colorado Psychodrama Centre.

Holmes, P. (1992). *The Inner World Outside: Object Relating Theory and Psychodrama.* London: Tavistock/Routledge.

Holmes, P., & Karp, M. (Eds.) (1991). *Psychodrama: Inspiration and Technique.* London: Tavistock/Routledge.

Holmes, P., Karp, M., & Watson, M. (Eds.) (1994). *Psychodrama Since Moreno: Innovations in Theory and Practice.* London and New York: Routledge.

Inger, I. B. (1993). A Dialogue Perspective for Family Therapy: The Contributions of Martin Buber and Gregory Bateson. *Journal of Family Therapy*, 15: 293–314.

Johnstone, K. (1979). *IMPRO. Improvisation and the Theatre*. London: Faber & Faber.

Jones, E. (1993). *Family Systems Therapy: Developments in the Milan-Systemic Therapies*. Chichester: John Wiley.

Kelly, G. A. (1955). *The Psychiatry of Personal Constructs* (two vols.). New York: W.W. Norton.

Keeney, B. P. (1983). *Aesthetics of Change*. New York: Guilford Press.

Keeney, B. P., & Ross, J. M. (1985). *Mind in Therapy: Constructing Systemic Family Therapies*. New York: Basic Books.

Kellermann, P. F. (1992). *Focus on Psychodrama: The Therapeutic Aspects of Psychodrama*. London: Jessica Kingsley.

Kipper, D. A. (1986). *Psychotherapy Through Clinical Role Playing*. New York: Brunner/Mazel.

Kobak, R. R., & Waters, D. B. (1984). Family Therapy as a Rite of Passage: Play's the Thing. *Family Process*, 23: 89–100.

Kohut, H. (1984). *How Does Analysis Cure?* Chicago, IL: University of Chicago Press.

Kreeger, L. (Ed.) (1975). *The Large Group*. London: Constable.

Laing, R. D. (1959). *The Divided Self*. London: Tavistock Publications.

Laing, R. D. (1967). Family and Individual Structure. In: Peter Lomas (Ed.), *The Predicament of the Family*. London: Hogarth Press.

Laing, R. D. (1969). *Self and Others*. London: Tavistock.

Langs, R. (1988). *A Primer of Psychotherapy*. New York: Gardner Press.

Lieberman, S. (1979). *Transgenerational Family Therapy*. London: Croom Helm.

Lerner, H. G. (1989). *The Dance of Intimacy*. New York: Harper & Row.

Mason, B. (1989). *Handing Over: Developing Consistency across Shifts in Residential and Health Settings*. London: D.C. Associates.

Maturana, H., & Varela, F. (1980). *Autopoesis and Cognition: The Realisation of the Living*. Dordrecht: Reidel.

Mead, G. H. (1934). *Mind, Self and Society*. Chicago, IL: University of Chicago Press.

Merquior, J. G. (1985). *Foucault*. London: Fontana Press.

Minuchin, S., & Fishman, H. C. (1981). *Family Therapy Techniques*. Cambridge, MA: Harvard University Press.

Moreno, J. L. (1937a). Inter-personal Therapy and the Psychopathology of Inter-personal Relations. *Sociometry, Vol. 1* (pp. 9–76). New York: Beacon House. Reprinted under the title "Psychopathology of Inter-personal Relations," in *Psychodrama, Vol. 1*. New York: Beacon House, 1946.

Moreno, J. L. (1937b). Sociometry in Relation to Other Social Services. *Sociometry, Vol. 1.* (pp. 206–219). New York: Beacon House. Also in: J. Fox (Ed.), *The Essential Moreno*. New York: Springer Publishing, 1987.

Moreno, J. L. (1940). Spontaneity and Cartharsis. In: Jonathon Fox (Ed.), *The Essential Moreno*. New York: Springer Publishing, 1987.

Moreno, J. L. (1953). Who Shall Survive? In: *Foundations of Sociometry, Group Psychotherapy and Sociodrama* (2nd ed.). Beacon, NY: Beacon House. (Also see "student edition", 1993, American Society of Group Psychotherapy and Psychodrama, McLean, VA.)

Moreno, Z. T. (1991). Time, Space, Reality, and the Family: Psychodrama with a Blended (Reconstituted) Family. In: P. Holmes & M. Karp (Eds.), *Psychodrama: Inspiration and Technique*. London: Tavistock/Routledge.

Penn, P. (1983). Circular Questioning. *Family Process, 3*: 267–280.

Pines, N. (Ed.) (1983). *The Evolution of Group Analysis*. London: Routledge & Kegan Paul.

Roberto, L. G. (1992). *Transgenerational Family Therapies*. New York: Guilford Press.

Symington, N. (1993). *Narcissism: A New Theory*. London: Karnac Books.

Telfner, U. (1991). The Epistemological Operations of Professionals. In: L. Fruggeri et al., *New Systemic Ideas from the Italian Mental Health Movement*. London: Karnac Books.

Tomm, K. (1987). Interventive Interviewing: Part II. Reflexive Questioning as a Means to Enable Self-Healing. *Family Process, 26*: 167–183.

Tomm, K. (1991). Personal communication. "Post-Milan Systemic Therapy." Workshop presented at Kensington Consultation Centre, London, November 19–20.

Von Foerster, H. (1979). Cybernetics of Cybernetics. In: K. Krippendorff (Ed.), *Communication and Control*. New York: Gordon & Beech.

Williams, A. (1989). *The Passionate Technique: Strategic Psychodrama with Individuals, Families, and Groups*. London: Routledge.

Williams, A. (1991). *Forbidden Agendas: Strategic Action in Groups*. London: Tavistock/Routledge.

Winnicott, D. W. (1962). Ego Integration in Child Development. In: *The Maturational Process and the Facilitating Environment*. London: The Hogarth Press and the Institute of Psychoanalysis. [Reprinted London: Karnac Books, 1990.]

Winnicott, D. W. (1974). *Playing and Reality*. Harmondsworth: Penguin. [Reprinted London: Karnac Books, 1991.]

Winnicott, D. W. (1965). *The Maturational Process and the Facilitating Environment*. London: The Hogarth Press and the Institute of Psychoanalysis. [Reprinted London: Karnac Books, 1990.]

INDEX